D1432419

WHAT PEOPLE ARE SAYING ABOUT
SELLING THROUGH RELATIONSHIPS

"What a fun, quick, and yet all-encompassing read! Stop struggling! Build a business you love. Today. Build an amazing business by building great relationships as Madewell describes in this beautiful blueprint for success."

MICHAEL J MAHER
International Bestselling Author, (7L) *The Seven Levels of Communication: Go from Relationships to Referrals* and Founder of The Generosity Generation.

SELLING THROUGH RELATIONSHIPS

WHY COLD CALLING SUCKS AND RELATIONSHIPS WIN

KATRINA MADEWELL

SELLING THROUGH RELATIONSHIPS
WHY COLD CALLING SUCKS AND RELATIONSHIPS WIN
BY KATRINA MADEWELL

To contact the author please visit KatrinaMadewell.com

Cover design, interior layout, and eBook by PearCreative.ca

ISBN (Print): 978-1-7361724-0-7

DEDICATION

To Shirley Jump: Thank you for helping me get through the writing process and pulling all that knowledge in my head out and into an organized fashion. I had so much fun creating this book with your help.

To Joe Stumpf: Thank you for encouraging me to be the highest and best version of myself. Through your work, you helped me transform into a version of myself I never thought possible. Your quest for knowledge and self-development is contagious to all of us around you. You have made my world an amazing place to be.

To Dave Ramsey: You have made millions of people debt free, including me. It changed my life, gave me freedom, and I finally have *choices*. Your message changed my being and the footprint I will leave on this world.

To my team: You guys show up with your A-Game, ready to play every day! The time, effort, and energy that goes into serving our clients at the highest level would not be possible without you.

To my work partners: You girls "get me". You see the vision and help me deliver a five-star experience to the people who trust us most. Everything WE do would be impossible without you.

To my husband Chris who built the strong foundation of our marriage and is an amazing spouse. You have been there through all of the best and worst of times, as well as everything in between. You always had my back and never left me and have remained always by my side. Life has been an incredible journey with you.

And most of all to my children: Tyler, Madalynne, Nicholas, and Adaleesa. I'm so proud of the incredible human beings you have become! You make a difference in the world, and it is because of you that I always strive to be better. My hope is to always, by example, teach you to be selfless people who are considerate of others and to be the gift to the world that you have been to me. I love you.

CONTENTS

FOREWORD

I chuckled when Katrina Madewell said, "Joe would you read the book and then write a foreword?"

I think Katrina knows that 80% of the people, who purchase or receive a book as a gift, will open the book. Only 45% get past the first 25 pages. A mere 20% will actually read the entire thing and of that 20%, only 5% will take notes and highlight the book.

I'm a 5% guy. I read it. I learned from it. I recommend it, and since you have it in your hands now, I'm going to encourage you to read it.

I'll try to make it easy for you to get started. Here are some of my highlights.

PAGE 16 — BE A SMART RESOURCE

I've known Katrina for 16 years. She's been a committed contributing member to By Referral Only, which is the largest community of agents in the world that are dedicated to building her business, based on the relationship vs. a transactional one, and Katrina is a legend in this world.

She engages in life and business with the Super Servants heart. Now this is not rhetoric, it's her way of being. The opposite of Super Servant is Super Star, that is an agent who focuses on shinning the light on themselves nonstop.

My direct experience after 16 years in relationship with Katrina, is that she's always leading with a giving hand focused on improving the lives of every person who crosses her path, and this book is just another example of that.

So read on…

PAGE 32 – MAKE SURE YOU HAVE TRUST

Katrina knows how much effort goes into building trust and she also has a deep realization of how easily trust can be broken. One way we build trust is to ask good questions followed up by great questions.

Throughout her book she gives you more than 50 thoughtful questions to deeply consider as you grow your wealth. I suggest you bring your highlighter with you as you look at page 32 through 38.

PAGE 43 – STABILITY

The model I've been teaching for more than 2 decades is the natural progression of the self-actualized person.

The progression is survival to stability, stability to success, success to significance and significance to scared.

I've been honored to watch Katrina Madewell make her journey to significance. She clearly communicates the essential guidance every person needs to create a stable platform upon which to build a successful and significant life. If creating wealth and developing deep relationships is important to you, then read page 43. You'll find yourself reading the next ten pages with ease.

Remember, "You can't give away what you don't got" and Katrina's got it. She is a self-made millionaire and she can show you exactly how to do it.

PAGE 93 – MAKE-UP SEX

This is where I started, you may want to do the same.

You'll find wise counsel that is very meaningful in today's complex world of creating agreement with others.

Katrina warns you of the difficulties a transaction has, but gives you great suggestions on how to minimize issues with her 'Promise Less – Deliver More' mindset.

That should get you started. It's time to read.

JOE STUMPF
ByReferralOnly.com
PrivateWork.com

INTRODUCTION

This book is a collection of thoughts, ideas, wisdom, and lessons, some of which took me years of learning the hard way, only to finally figure out a better way to build my business than day-to-day cold calling. Sure, you can get customers that way but, I assure you, you'll love selling your product or service far better when you know the people in your target market and show up, every day, with the heart of a super servant first and a salesperson last. Always do what is right and the rest will follow.

In this book, you will discover how my experience and background helped me build a net worth of over a million dollars. While this is not as much money as it used to be, getting there was an uphill journey for me, and is one that I built on my own without gifts or handouts from anyone. I wanted to share what I learned so you can do it too, all without cold calling or knocking on doors. Make no mistake, you have to start somewhere but you want to quickly move out of this sales cycle and into wealth-building, so use this book as your blueprint.

My stories in my real estate career will help you understand how to build a customer base that you can count on so that you don't have to be that "stranger sales-person" pounding the streets to drum up business.

My guiding questions will help lead you through how your organization operates, who your customer is, how to improve the experience, and how to gain and retain repeat and referred customers who trust you, so that you have those relationships for life.

Whether you are single or married for decades, like me, you will relate to my stories and examples. My hope is that you shorten the learning curve for building and growing a strong relationship that will outlive you and leave a legacy behind for generations to come.

Finally, I truly hope you discover your big WHY and let it be the guiding principle in everything you do so that you make a huge impact on the world.

CHAPTER ONE

THE ATTRACTION PHASE

"Why are you here?"

That's one of the first questions I ask every prospective client when each of us is getting to know the other and deciding whether we can *and should* work together. Perhaps I ask it a little more tactfully, but basically, that's it. It's a lot like when you first meet a potential date. You don't know the other person that well, so you ask a few questions to gather more information before you make a decision to even continue the conversation, go out to dinner, or simply move on and find someone more suitable. In business, we engage the same way.

It's the dance of connection, knowledge, need, and trust; and, if we're smart, we're doing it because we are looking to build a lifelong relationship with our clients and customers.

> Trust and connection are the cornerstones to building lifelong client relationships.

Too many business owners, however, are focused on the bottom line. They get that one deal closed and then, after the sale, leave that relationship to flounder if they ever bothered to foster it at all. By creating a true connection with your clients and customers, followed by an innate desire to serve them from *their perspective* (some call this meeting them where they are), you set up your business for even more success. Many of my clients have returned over and over again for decades and refer me to others, including their children. They know I genuinely care about them and that I always focus on meeting their needs instead of worrying solely about profit margins.

THE BEGINNINGS OF THE RELATIONSHIP

I don't know if I found the real estate and mortgage business or if it found me. Like it was yesterday, I remember the first house my mother bought when I was twelve and the emotions we both felt that day. The house wasn't much better than the apartment we had been living in, but it was a huge achievement for my mother. It was a home, a place we could call our own, something we never had living in a rental. I realized, even then, how important homeownership was and how important having a sense of one's own space could be. Simply the ability to plant your own garden or paint the walls whatever color you want has a huge impact on a person's life and it dramatically affects children's lives, too. It's an unspoken truth: You don't have to unwillingly move when it's *your* home. You have control over how long you stay and, in general, can control rising housing costs.

When I was fourteen, I got my first job at Chick-fil-A. I will never forget how the manager, Bill, interviewed me. I could feel that he wanted to give me a shot but knew he was concerned I might be too young. "If I hire you, how will you get to and from work?" he asked me.

I replied, "Mr. Bill, if you will give me a shot, I will be here when I am supposed to be. I'll be on time, and I'll do the best job possible for you and your customers." I didn't just want the job, I wanted to immerse myself in the culture of Chick-fil-A. This family-owned business franchise has some of the strongest core values of any company I've seen. They insist on a day of rest to serve God. They're focused on filling customers' needs and delivering an experience that is second to none. This fast food chain has less turnover and does more business in six days than McDonalds does in seven. Part of their mission is to have a positive influence on everyone they come into contact with. They certainly did with me.

Bill gave me my first opportunity to earn money. More importantly, he taught me how to serve a customer at a high level and how to anticipate the customers' needs without having them ask. Have you ever noticed that you never have to ask for a straw or napkins when you go through a Chickfil-A drive-through? They have always been ahead of the curve.

They added double drive-throughs and order takers before they were needed. Even if there is a line around the building, their customers will wait because they know what to expect. Lines move quickly and orders are correct because that's the standard they've set. According to various business journals, Chick-fil-A has an order accuracy of 91.6%. Other chains have an average 87.2% accuracy. Their customers are loyal because Chick-fil-A regularly delivers beyond expectations. All businesses could learn a lot from the Chickfil-A's customer service model. I know I sure did.

My first job in the industry was with a mortgage company that served a lot of people with subpar credit. The next job was one of those turn-and-burn, answer-the-phone, get-the-loan-done, and move-on-to-the-next-customer type of company. Looking back, I think God put me in those two companies to learn both sides of the business along with a few hard lessons. Within a few years of purchasing our "American dream" home, the first house my husband and I bought was over-mortgaged. Coupled with a bad economy and rates over 7%, we were forced to do a short sale, years before short sales were even a "thing". As a mortgage broker, I was humiliated that I lost my own home. I didn't want anyone to know I had failed at the one thing I was helping other people do.

That terrifying and stressful event gave me humility and I learned three things:

1. To be better with money and follow the dreaded B word: a budget

2. To teach people not to use their homes like an ATM

3. To help other people find and hold onto their home and their equity while ultimately building wealth

I began to change how I handled things at work by spending more time on the phone with customers. The rest of the office was grind, grind, grind, and get that next mortgage deal done. I simply couldn't operate that way, especially after going through that short sale. My empathy for our customers who desperately needed a mortgage solution shifted my focus and I began to ask questions. More importantly, I learned to take time to *listen*.

> **In my first few years in the industry, I learned one of the best leadership skills: ACTIVE LISTENING.**

I remember a customer named Ron who had seen our advertisement in the newspaper. This was pre-internet and he'd called the office looking to refinance at the lowest possible rate. We got to talking about his home and his goals. Over the course of several phone calls, we built a friendship. He was into computers and reminded me of my uncle and grandfather because he was so tech-savvy. He introduced me to the concept of email, which was brand-new back then. After his refinance was completed, he sent me flowers. It was the first time a customer ever did that and it touched my heart.

He told me he was grateful that I had seen him as a person, not a transaction. He said he felt a connection between us and knew it was one of care, compassion, and that I was someone who put my customer's needs first.

> See clients as people. Not as transactions.

Soon after that, I went into business for myself. I worked in too many mortgage shops where relationships with the customers were not part of the culture. They only cared about the numbers and volume, and I wanted to do things differently.

> You can create the culture you want in your own business when you don't agree with the culture you're in.

GETTING TO KNOW EACH OTHER

When I first branched out on my own, I took out some advertisements and did the traditional things to make the phone ring. At the same time, I concentrated on finding customers within the network I had already built. I worked within my existing sphere and expanded from there. There were so many people with whom I previously had several conversations and now they were ready to sell/buy/refinance a house. Even though it might be a few years before they were ready, I made time to sit down with potential clients over coffee or dinner so we could get to know each other. The *very* first impression and the impact of that moment are the memories you will leave with that customer. This will determine your relationship in the future, especially as technology evolves and some jobs, and those who do them, will be eliminated. You don't want to be in the eliminated category.

> It's true what they say:
> First impressions are the most important.

When I was pregnant with my first child, Madalynne, I had terrible morning sickness and spent many days feeling miserable. At the time, I was working with a lady in Miami and my morning sickness was so bad that I didn't return her calls for several days. When I finally connected with her, I apologized and explained what was going on. Most people would be pissed about their broker dropping off the radar in the middle of a new construction deal. However, because I had built a relationship based on trust, she didn't get angry. In fact, she sent flowers to congratulate me on her upcoming birth.

In those days, I didn't have the staff I have today. I was the chef and chief bottle-washer, and when the rainmaker is down for a few days, the work piles up like a snowball going downhill. It was just as vital then as it is now to build those relationships founded on trust and shared goals.

Every time I've lost a client, it has crushed me. I'm a little paralyzed for a moment because I want to figure out what went wrong or how I could have done better. Sometimes you just don't click with a client or their goals change and they move on. Some are just in it for the dollars and cents and I know it's not personal.

> Sometimes you just don't click with a client, or their goals change and they move on... I know it's not personal.

BUILD THE CONNECTION ON THE RIGHT FOUNDATION

Before you can build a house, you have to pour a solid foundation. That base is formed from a few key concepts:

KNOW YOUR WHY

WHY ARE YOU IN THIS INDUSTRY?

It's a simple question that can sometimes have a complicated answer. Think about that for a moment. Why did you choose your industry? I didn't choose the real estate industry because I wanted to be rich. I chose it because I wanted to help people find and protect their most precious asset—their home—and give them a great experience during the process, one that exceeded their expectations. I know how important that is and how scary it is to lose your home. My *why* is bigger than one sale, and yours should be, too.

HAVE YOUR BIG VISION

Ask yourself: *What do I see for the future?* Sit down and dream big about what kind of business you want and then write down your answers to the following questions:

- What market(s) do you want to serve?

- Who will your ideal customer be?

- Where do you want to be in five years, ten years, and twenty years?

- How will your customer base evolve?

As you're building your team, find the right people who fit, who believe in your vision and can fulfill your mission statement. I constantly look for people who can be a proactive part of my vision, which means we are all on the same page and that helps the whole company keep moving in the right direction, one that aligns with my big vision. They are here to be a part of something bigger than themselves, not just for a job. They have a big spot to fill and their roles matter.

KEYS TO SUCCESS

Build a great customer relationship by asking the questions that determine your customer's needs and how you can help them. Sometimes it's not a match. In that case, refer the person to someone else and be honest about why this might not be the right time for you two to work together. Even if they ultimately go with someone else, people will remember you started from a place of empathy and that you weren't just in it for a sale. That's a relationship that endures.

KNOW YOUR CUSTOMERS' WHY

Next, ask yourself: *Why are my customers here?* What do your customers need and want? What drove them to you? For instance, I was talking to a woman from Wisconsin who was looking for a house in the Tampa Bay area. Another realtor might assume she was just one more snowbird, but I quickly realized there was a much larger reason she was willing to move across country from a state with long winters to a state that was pretty summer all year 'round. People always start with "I want a three-bedroom, two-bathroom home at X price", but my job is really to uncover what they truly want and why they are moving. People don't just wake up and say, "I'm going to move to Florida today." There is always a reason why they started thinking about moving.

Instead of shooting off a bunch of listings, I asked this woman to tell me about herself and why she wanted to move to Florida. She told me about her adult children and how imperative it was to live here and help raise her grandchildren. Her *why* was personal and important to her. Knowing that, I found the perfect place where she could fulfill her vision of the future *It's not just about selling a house.*

> What's your Why? Know *your* Why.
> Know *your customers'* Why.

I've never met a buyer or seller who randomly decided to buy or sell a home. There's always something going on, some driving force behind that decision. If you come in and tell me you want to sell your house, I'm not going to start with the paperwork. I'm going to ask you the story of your home and why you made the appointment. Together, we will craft a plan for your future home sale. There is some reason why you have been thinking of selling, and there is a reason you called me; something happened to trigger the thought of moving.

If I can clarify your values early on, every choice and decision we make along the way will be so much easier. Most importantly, everything we do will be based on the things you said were most important to you. Maybe you just had a child and now you want your own home, need a bigger space, better schools, etc. Those facts are the beginning of the conversation.

At my company, we go deep to uncover important details, like a young couple being the first in their family to buy their own home. Or a military family who isn't just looking for a home, but rather a stable foundation for their kids because they are sick of their family moving every two years. Those are really important factors that don't come out on their own. It takes time to talk with customers to discover important details that really matter.

It's these deeper conversations where we grow the roots of our relationship because I really *know* my customers, their family, and I took the time to help them from a place of true understanding.

> Anyone can show up and sell a house,
> but I'm not just "Anyone".

MEET THE CUSTOMERS' NEEDS

When you talk to your customers, you should be asking: *What do you need right now?* In the more than thirty years I've been in this industry, I have so many stories about clients who were in a desperate situation when they reached out to me, like Jenny, a former mortgage client who called me one day in a panic. Her husband had died years earlier and due to some bad legal advice, her house was in foreclosure. She called me to sell it, but I knew, after talking to her, that she really called me looking for options. Years and years earlier, I told Jenny to call me if she ever needed anything, something I tell every client, and she remembered that. I could have done the easy thing and sold her house. Instead, I helped her find a good attorney and lender. She initially hired a bad attorney who gave her horrible legal advice and she was on the brink of losing her home. I helped her save it, even though my company wasn't going to make any money. My only goal was to connect her with the right people. One thing I'm sure of— when the time is right for her to sell, I will be the agent she picks because she knows I have her best interests at heart.

> It's not all about the sale.

I had another first-time homebuyer, Robert. He was a single dad with two kids whose family had been living in a camper. He was looking for a modest first home on a tight budget. He didn't fit the usual market we serve, but I could hear the need in his voice and managed to find a great deal in a good neighborhood where he could raise his kids. We even helped him obtain some down payment assistance and he settled in with his children.

A couple of years later, he called again wanting to sell it. I was shocked because the house had been so perfect and was such a great bargain. I asked him why he wanted to sell the home we worked so hard to buy. It turned out he wasn't looking to actually sell—he had lost his job and was scared he couldn't afford his mortgage anymore. We talked about where he had worked when he bought the home and he told me that his position was terminated, leaving him unemployed. I talked with him to see if there were any other new opportunities for him. He told me there were, including a job he had already been offered but he needed his CDL license to work there. The problem was he couldn't afford the class.

I paid for his CDL classes because it was an easy thing I could do that would make a tremendous difference in his and his children's lives. In the end, we landed in a very different place from Robert's initial call saying, "Hey, I want to put my house up and see what I can get for it". You might think that after my last two stories that I just reject sales, but the truth is I sell a lot and I am referred over 90% of the time.

> It's the little things that make a huge difference.

BE A SMART RESOURCE

What's your long-term goal? Much of my days are spent educating people about the time value of money (what a dollar can buy today isn't what it will buy in the future), along with how to build long-term wealth through real estate. I don't want any of my clients to end up house-poor because that's setting them up to fail. They could buy too much house and find themselves in foreclosure a few years later. I talk to them about debt and eliminating it, about not using their house's equity as an ATM, and about the value of real estate and that keeping rental real estate is a long-term wealth option.

I care enough to make sure they aren't house-poor. I'm not lecturing them but I'm always coming from a place of love with a servant's heart. If I didn't tell you that I cringe when I see people renting, living paycheck to paycheck, with car payments larger than their house payment, I would be remiss. Unfortunately, it happens more than it should.

> With a servant's heart, I educate my clients
> about wealth building through real estate.
> It's not just about buying a house.

AVOID COMMISSION BREATH

This is more than a transaction to me. People know when they are being "sold" to. They'll buy things if they need them, want them, or if it will take a pain point away, but they don't want a salesperson with commission breath breathing down their neck. They can sense if an agent is trying to sell a home so the agent can pay their own mortgage. A customer knows, deep down, if the recommendations and advice are based on the agent's needs instead of the customer's. They can *feel* it.

BUILDING A FOREVER BUSINESS

If you want customer relationships that will last for decades, start with the three basic traits of attraction:

Confidence

Empathy

Transparency

Be real, be true, and be honest—always. You won't just build a great business that way, you'll also build a great and satisfying life for yourself. Knowing you are being your best self in your company will bring you a joy no amount of money can buy.

If you know your product inside and out, that inner confidence will show and be attractive to potential clients. That confidence is the difference between going on a date with someone who is exciting, fun to talk to, and who has good energy, and sitting down for an endless coffee with someone who barely interacts and keeps looking at their phone or watch. Or worse, someone who only talks about themselves.

Likeability is just as important as confidence. People are attracted to and want to work with people they like. Customers want to feel like you understand and care about them. You cultivate that by being fully present when you are talking to them. You don't check your phone every five seconds; you don't let your mind wander to what's for dinner. In my industry, people are coming to me with their biggest purchase or sale of their largest asset, and in most cases their mortgage is also their largest liability, and the things that matter deeply to them, and they need to know I'm invested in the outcome, too.

> Likeability is just as key as confidence.

I've used the same car dealer for the last three or four cars because the salesperson, Scott, understands what I want and need, how my cars will be used, and what kind of factors matter in the automobiles I intend to buy. I trust him so implicitly and have negotiated and bought cars over the phone. I've also dealt with dealerships that didn't listen to me when I told them what I wanted, weren't available when I needed an answer, and had such a fast turnover of people that I never spoke to the same person twice. In fact, car salespeople turn over at 67%!

No customer wants to feel like they're just another number in a high-volume store. They want to know you care about them and their needs. The car dealerships that sell through relationships outlast the ones that have regular turn over. Think about it—car salespeople have a constant turnover rate, with most rarely lasting more than one year and a whopping 40% of them won't even last ninety days! Yet research shows most people change cars every six years. While numbers and profit matter, the salespeople work at good dealerships that build that all-important trust factor and that are genuinely interested in their customers, not just their bottom line.

Scott has been at Toyota for over ten years, and in their service department, Rick has been there for over fourteen years. Not only do I like them, I trust them, and they know their product and they know me! It's because of this that I continue to buy from them and have my cars serviced there. It's also why I go out of my way to refer others to them. I know what I am getting, and it isn't someone merely trying to sell me something.

> Building trust and taking genuine interest
> in your client makes all the difference when
> you're building a forever business.

Too much of the real estate industry has been focused on finding the cheapest, next best solution. There is no sustainability in that business model as you'll be easily replaced by the next cheap solution. When you think about something as large and expensive as a home, it's foolish to trust the transfer of this asset to the cheapest solution you find in that moment.

Trust, however, is a limited commodity. People will pay for exceptional service, value, and knowledge, as well as a relationship that is considerate and built on reliability. That is the kind of foundation that creates word-of-mouth referrals, no matter what industry you are in. There's nothing more attractive to a potential client than a businessperson who is genuine and already loved by others.

CHAPTER TWO

THE FIRST DATES

Have you ever been on a date where it felt like you were listening to the same resume for the hundredth time? What do you do for work? Where did you grow up? How many kids do you have? You're yawning before the waitress takes your order. Imagine, however, if your date opened with a question like, *Tell me about your greatest adventure.*

That's the kind of interaction that creates interest and good conversation. You go home from the date intrigued and wondering when you'll see that person again because they were different—and most importantly, truly interested in you.

With any real estate transaction or business dealing, it's the same thing. Most start a conversation with, *"What are you looking for? How many bedrooms? Baths? School district?"* It's boring, isn't it? We don't start our conversations that way.

IT'S ABOUT MORE THAN BEDS AND BATHS

When I sit down with a new client, my main goal is to get to know the person and uncover their needs, at a deep level—it's the most important thing I'll do. I start by enquiring about where they want to go from here or how they arrived at the decision to even set up the meeting with me. I don't want to start with questions that result in yes or no answers. I ask open-ended questions that begin to build the skeleton of a relationship with my client.

It is just as important they get to know me as much as I'm getting to know them. We are feeling each other out, testing the waters and making sure the fit is right. There are some agents who meet prospective new clients at a bar and sign a listing agreement an hour later, as if it's a one-night stand. It's mortifying to hear some of the ways people have met their agent and jumped right into a transaction with someone they barely knew. We aren't that kind of Realtor®.

Our first consultation is oftentimes an hour long. We understand people are busy and some might see an hour as too long or a timewaster, but it's the exact opposite. Buying and/or selling a house is one of the biggest transactions you will have in your life. It's not something you should rush into with the first person you meet at an open house who happens to have a real estate license. Yet so many people do just that.

It's like eloping with the first match you get on a dating site. You would never do that, would you?

DON'T BE NEEDY

I've been married for almost twenty-five years now, but a long time ago I dated a guy who was constantly asking me if we were okay, if I was mad at him, or if I knew where our relationship was going. He was insecure and needy, and I was done within a few dates. Imagine if you're a customer with a needy Realtor® who is desperate to sell your house so he can pay his own mortgage (remember the whole concept of commission breath? That applies here, too).

When I met my husband, I was in a place where I didn't need or even really want a relationship. That only seemed to attract him more because I wasn't hanging on his every phone call. I was carving out a life of my own and wasn't stressing over whether he was going to be a part of it or not. People who are needy repel others, both in dating and in business. You need to be able to enter into a transaction confident and secure in the knowledge that you bring tremendous value to the table.

> When you know your worth,
> it shows and attracts clients like a magnet.

That push-pull of magnetism sometimes works in reverse when you stand firm in your boundaries and values when working with clients. Recently, I had a buyer named Don who had worked with me for a month or so. He found a house and made a ridiculously low offer that was insulting to the seller. I pulled him aside and told him it was really important to me that he had an amazing experience working with us, however I didn't feel like he was letting me lead and guide him through the process. I was ready to walk away and let him find another Realtor® who wouldn't push back when he was going down a road that would end badly. He had already pissed off the seller to the point of where the seller did not want to accept any offer from him. My team watched as I attempted to terminate this relationship. Don was a first-time home buyer armed with Google research. While I appreciated his researching and gaining knowledge to avoid making huge mistakes, I was there to protect him from making unnecessary missteps and guide him to making a great decision that would be a win-win for all parties involved.

He respected my stance and "felt" my intention to terminate and discontinue the relationship. In fact, I was very frank about it. Instead of leaving, he decided to take my advice. He understood that we were in this together. A few weeks later, he owned his dream house with his wife and we had another satisfied buyer. It shows when you care more about the customer's experience and their success than a paycheck and they are more likely to respect your honesty and expertise.

KEYS TO SUCCESS

When you build a home, you don't start with the blueprint—you start with the core foundational pieces like the soil, the moisture barrier, the view, the long-term growth of the area. The same is true for your business and any other long-term relationship.

DATE WIDELY AT FIRST

Most people who start dating don't pick one person and leap into a long-term relationship. Especially when we're younger and we don't yet know what kind of person fits us best, most people date widely and find their "type". The same is true in business. Why would you sign with the very first agent you meet? This is a massive financial transaction and it's important to interview multiple agents to find the one who best aligns with your goals. This is a big decision that you should not leave to chance and once you have a relationship with someone and you know each other well, there's no need to date again. After all, isn't dating the hardest part in finding the perfect mate?

> You wouldn't marry someone after only one date, would you? Same with real estate agents. Don't commit to one after only a single short meeting.

I once had a client whose only question was what I charged. I explained my commission rate is standard and that the more important question he should be asking is what I planned to deliver for that commission? What set me apart from the other agents he was considering? What would my agency offer that another company might not? How are we different and how will that uniqueness play into his goals?

Real estate is one of the only industries in a world that operates 100% on contingency and without a retainer. We invest all of our time, money, resources, marketing efforts, and leverage our connections upfront, with no definite guarantee of a sale. We don't get paid a dime until we bring you a contract and finalize all of your closing details and it's a funded deal, so your agent should be working hard for you from day one. Here's a little hint, an agent asking those questions in advance will help you weed out the ones who just want a check and won't go the extra mile.

KNOW WHAT YOU DON'T WANT

When you buy your first home and live in it for a little while, you figure out what you don't want in your next house and what you can't live without. Maybe that open floor plan that looked so pretty is noisy with three toddlers underfoot. Maybe the updated and charming, yet tiny, kitchen no longer fits with your newfound passion for baking. When you know better, you choose better, and every house going forward will be better aligned with what you want.

> ## When you know better, you choose better.

It's the same thing with choosing a real estate agent. I actually got into real estate because I had such a terrible experience buying my own house that I decided to go into the industry and become everything the agents selling real estate were not. If you had a bad experience with your agent, you would go out of your way to avoid that same experience in the future. Determine what qualities you do and don't want in the people you work with and use that criteria during the interview and selection process.

DON'T COMMIT TOO SOON

The National Association of Realtors statistics show that over 75% of people buy or sell with the first agent they meet. When it comes to something as important as a home purchase or home sale, it's vital that you take your time and don't leap into a real estate relationship with the first agent who hands you a business card. This is going to be your biggest asset, your biggest purchase, and your highest monthly payment. You'll also be incurring a huge liability (debt) if you have a mortgage, so your choice should reflect that importance. Most of the time these agents you are meeting in the field and along the way might either be new or only looking to gain a customer.

While that's okay, just understand the agent with the most knowledge and wherewithal is not going to be the one sitting in an open house. Don't get me wrong, new people have to start somewhere but, knowing what I know now, I am looking for the expert who can and will lead, guide, and protect me in what will likely be the largest purchase or asset of my life.

DON'T GET TOO DEEP TOO FAST

Just as you wouldn't go from the first date to *I love you* before midnight, you shouldn't get too deeply invested with a home or an agent until you are positive they right for you. You could sign a contract, then realize a couple weeks down the road that the person you are working with doesn't have the habits, knowledge, or experience you were looking for. My negotiating skills are worth every penny I am paid, and you don't want to discover someone doesn't have those negotiating teeth in the middle of a transaction. It could cost you thousands of dollars if they make a mistake or lack the knowledge that a seasoned agent, like me, with years of experience and thousands of transactions under their belt will bring to you. The agent should always be your ally and always have your best interests at heart—not his or her own agenda.

By choosing the right agent, you can concentrate on your own life and career that make you money and not have to worry about every detail of the process. Someone with experience and good communication skills will lead and guide you through the process so you can focus on your job and family. The agent should be honest and transparent, even if they are telling you things you don't want to hear. Listen closely because that is a good sign that you are in the right hands. A good agent will be upfront about pricing, the current market, and comps of what other homes are actually SELLING for, and help you make decisions that are focused on the goals you set in the initial meeting.

CHAPTER THREE

DISAPPOINTMENT

Here's a harsh fact—people are going to let you down. They're going to disappoint you, make you mad, and not be there when you need them most. That's true of relationships, both personal and business. The key is to make sure your client's expectations, and what you can actually deliver to them, are a good match, and realistic.

DON'T BE EVERYTHING TO EVERYONE

When I first started in this industry, I decided that I wanted to be the kind of Realtor® to whom other people referred regularly. I wanted to be an invaluable resource, and to build great experiences for my clients. For me, it's never been about trying to attract every single potential homebuyer or seller, because not everyone is a good fit for me. Likewise, I may not be the best match for them. That's part of what makes us different—we don't work with everyone.

I would rather say to someone, "You know, I just don't think we're going to be a good match," than to continue the working relationship and end up disappointing them because our personalities don't mesh or the clients have completely unrealistic expectations. Yes, their business will go to someone else but chances are the other firm will be the one to disappoint the impossible-to-please client; but it won't be me.

Most importantly, however, is that you keep the promises you make. Ask yourself (and answer honestly):

Do you do what you say you're going to do?

Do you deliver on what you promise?

Can the client rely on you to be true to your brand and your words?

That old adage to under-promise and over-deliver will go a long way in building repeat customers and having your own tribe of loyal customers.

> Keep the promises you make.

MAKE SURE YOU HAVE TRUST

A really good metaphor for disappointment in business relationships is seeing someone's picture on a dating site and think it looks great. You chat with them over the messaging program, set up a date, and the person who walks into the restaurant doesn't match their twenty-years-and-twenty-plus-pounds-ago picture. Before the waitress even hands you a menu, you subconsciously don't trust that person because they haven't been truthful and upfront in their marketing. This same principle applies to business.

That trust is just as important in business as it is in your personal life. Don't make promises you don't intend to keep. Be who you are, be clear about what you will deliver, and make sure you communicate well and often. Otherwise, if the dots aren't connecting for the client in those initial meetings, they will start to distrust you and that can undermine the professional relationship. This is an important point to keep in mind whether you are launching your own business, running a small business that already understands and applies these principles, or you're looking to take your organization to the next level and grow your business.

> Trust is important in personal and business relationships. Be who you are in all circumstances.

As I've said before, your home is your biggest purchase, your biggest asset, and your biggest monthly payment. It's essential that you trust the person who is helping you buy or sell that home. As I have said to many people over the years, if that person isn't me, that's fine—just be sure to find someone you can and do trust implicitly.

Trust and honesty go hand in hand in relationship building so I'm honest about the cause and effect of the client's choices as well. For example, someone who doesn't want to stage their house needs to understand they probably won't get the highest and best price in the shortest amount of time. Kim, our home stager, will attest to the fact that our staged homes sell faster and for higher prices than people who choose not to stage their home. It's also true that sellers who don't make their properties available for showings on the buyer's timeline often risk losing a sale. Whatever the option, is the decision you've made worth it to you in the long run?

> Trust and honesty go hand in hand
> when building relationships.

In today's world, people operate on demand and on their own timeline, so it's important that your business can meet the customer as their time demands. It's possible to do this and yet still have a system in place that operates within your own boundaries. For example, I take every Sunday off. It's been my only day off for years. You can be like Chick-fil-A and set the expectation from the beginning that you will be closed on Sunday. Chick-Fil-A customers aren't mad that they are closed for the day, they respect the boundaries of the business model that has been set up by Chick-fil-A and they are consistent. In other words, Chick-fil-A would never open on a Sunday just because business is in a slump, but they may choose to extend their hours the other six days. Regardless, they are consistently closed on Sundays and their customers know it. If you have set the expectation with your customers that you are closed on certain days, your loyal customers will respect your boundaries and work within them because they choose to work with you.

> Create boundaries around your time.

I also trust that my clients will communicate with me if they're unhappy. In that initial consultation, I ask them to leave me a review towards the end of the transaction. Furthermore, if at any point along the way they feel the review will be anything less than five stars, I ask them to let me know about it immediately and give us the opportunity to fix the issue.

I'm not afraid to have those conversations upfront about being human and that it's possible for people to make mistakes or for there to be miscommunication. What you don't want is to be blindsided by this at the end of the transaction. This approach and transparency increase the trust in my relationships with clients. It's on me if I don't have those conversations about the tough issues upfront and I can't be upset if I get a negative review later.

BE CLEAR FROM THE START

We have a policy of being clear with our clients at that very first consultation. I want to be upfront and honest—in fact, we show them and say things like, *here are the eighty-eight kinds of turbulence you could possibly encounter and you may*

experience one or more of them during a real estate transaction.
Actually, after almost thirty years in this industry, I can make
that list a hundred and eighty-eight things. There are so many
things that can go wrong, delay, or ruin the deal and/or the
customer experience. The unfortunate truth is that so many of
those things are beyond my control.

Clients need to know what's possible upfront to avoid
disappointment or confusion later. It's the same concept when
a doctor is going to prescribe a new medicine or do surgery.
There are always possible complications and things that the
physician can't control. The key is to clearly communicate
these things to the patient in advance, while being the trusted
guide with the other details that are going into the whole
scenario. By communicating all of this upfront, not only will
it prepare the patient should there be any complications but it
also gives them the opportunity to ask questions so they feel
good about the procedure. By communicating in detail, the
patient knows the risks and avoids surprises. Let's face it, most
people hate or fear the unknown and will avoid unwanted
surprises. It can make them scared or paralyze them with fear,
even though the outcome is often worth the risk.

> Err on the side of over-communicating with your clients.

Too many times, I've met clients who had no idea what to
expect because their agent wasn't upfront with them. They
came to us because they felt let down when things went awry

and their agent didn't communicate clearly with them. April and Rhett were a couple who needed to buy and sell their current home on the same day because all of their cash was tied up in their home's equity. This is called a simultaneous close, and it comes with a lot of risk and many things that we can't control. We made sure to take a lot of extra time to explain what would happen, as well as what *could* happen.

Later in this transaction, unfortunately during the very week they were set to close, the buyer lost his job. In an instant, the whole plan fell apart which was something far beyond our control. However, we had talked to the clients early on to let them know that if anything changed in the plan, like there was a loss of income on any side, everything could change. Because we discussed what could go wrong, they took the delay in stride and were prepared to switch gears. The couple was able to borrow the money to cover the gap while we restaged and relisted their home. A month later, we found another buyer and moved to close quickly.

The point is that blow would have been substantially worse *(in a situation that neither of us could do anything about)* had we not discussed the risks and pitfalls in advance. The fact remains that, because we did, we were able to manage the client's expectations and get back on track without the customer being disappointed or blaming us for the snafu. They knew we were by their side every step of the way, no matter what. We already had a back-up plan; their primary goal was to get them into a larger home because they had seriously outgrown the home they were in. Reminding people of what is important to them about the decision to buy or sell, using their own words, keeps the focus on the end result and not anything happening in the middle.

WHEN YOU HAVE TO DELIVER BAD NEWS

In real estate, our motto is location, location, location. But in business, I believe it should be communication, communication, communication. That has to be the most important part of your client relationships. If you start out with honest and thorough communication, your clients will be prepared for detours in the road ahead. One of the questions I ask people in advance is what their expectations are from me as their Realtor®. So many people say communication, because they want to be kept in the loop.

> Communication! Communication! Communication!
> I can't stress this enough.

When something goes awry, don't procrastinate communicating with your client—but *do* take a moment to figure out a backup plan before you pick up the phone. I think through the process and try to strategize a good plan B *before* I make that call. Together, we explore all our options to keep things on track. That is, after all, what they are paying me to do—to watch their backs and guide them through a confusing, difficult, and stressful process when emotions are naturally already high.

I often take a day to gather some facts and figures, talk to some people so I can gather facts and explore our options, then I call the client and the other agent. We can avoid a lot of panicked decisions that way and come to the table with a solution instead of a problem.

Delivering bad news is never fun but go by the old adage—rip off the band-aid right away. Then be there to help them clean the wound once you do; it's going to hurt, so we simply help them focus and breathe. Don't be afraid to lean into the bad news. It's about transparency, and again, it all goes back to not avoiding those difficult conversations.

KEYS TO SUCCESS

Maintaining trusting relationships with your clients is easy if you are open and flexible, and do the following:

1. Communicate with honesty
2. Have a Plan B ready to go if things go wrong
3. Lean into difficult conversations; don't avoid them
4. Know what's important to your client and meet those needs

Above all, communicate in a language your client can understand. Doctors are often so afraid of malpractice suits that they really watch what they say. They'll dump a bunch of medical-lingo options in your lap and ask you to make a decision. The average person doesn't understand that lingo and needs someone to help guide them through the pros and cons. If my doctor gives me options for something and I don't *really* understand the implications, I'm never afraid to ask, "If I was your wife, what would you advise *her* to do?"

They are the expert in this field not me, so I am looking for that balance of knowledge, trust, advice, and guidance. I don't want a physician to be vague in their answers to avoid a malpractice suit. By leaning into and building a relationship early on and over time, I can ask a more personal question like, "Knowing what you know, what would you advise your wife to do?".

In my opinion, doctors get into trouble when they treat people like products in an assembly line instead of treating them like family. This used to be called a good bedside manner. The ones who have this trust with their patients, and come from a place of understanding, care, and compassion, are by far at less risk of being sued. After all, who really sues family and friends? Sometimes you just have to slow down and engage in the situation to come from a place of service, not a sale. Somehow, physicians and businesses have lost sight of the fact that there is a human on the other end who wants to be treated as a person, not a replaceable commodity. Just as I work to build relationships of trust with my clients, I look for doctors and other service professionals that will take that necessary and extra time upfront to access the full situation. This simple action leads to trust over a long period of time.

Sometimes you just have to slow down and engage in the situation to come from a place of service instead of a sale.

When things don't go well, I rarely get disappointed. I have found that, nine times out of ten, if a transaction doesn't close usually it was in the best interest of the client. I talk the clients through it and make sure they understand what's happening and what the ramifications are. By the same token, I don't want them to regret a purchase so communicating with them about potential issues down the road can allow the client to make an informed decision. They feel like they are part of the family, which is important to me.

I see people in real estate, as well as other industries, who get upset when things don't go their way. That's unproductive and only gets you mired in a negative space. My husband and I recently bought a used truck. While we negotiated a good deal at a dealership we had used in the past, we also told the salesman we wanted to look around and see if we could find another truck with less miles.

The second place we went to had a truck with lower miles but the salesperson was huffy and annoyed that we were trying to negotiate the best deal for us and our pre-set budget. He acted like we were wasting his time. I reminded him that this truck had to work for me, not for him. His attitude was a real turn-off and we ultimately returned to the first dealership where we previously purchased several vehicles. They were happy to see us return and threw in an extended warranty with the deal, making the truck a much better option for us. They handled it well and we were happy to give them return business.

We were very transparent about what we were looking for (lower miles at the same price with lots of upgrades) and that we were looking around to get the best bang for our buck. Typically we make decisions quickly, but we compared many trucks over a short period of time and made the best decision in that moment. It is important to note that we don't take months or even weeks to make a decision; just enough time to be comfortable with our due diligence.

With every client, I will always spend more time on the front end so that the entire purchase and sales process goes smoother. I don't want to pressure anyone or leave a client feeling like they're making these big decisions alone or in a rush. If you set the expectations correctly from the start, everything will work out better. Unrealistic expectations, on either side, will kill you in a relationship and in a business transaction.

> If you set expectations correctly from the start, everything will work out better.

CHAPTER FOUR

STABILITY

When I consider the word stability, I think of the foundational pieces of a home. It brings to mind things like the ground you choose to build on and the slab that becomes the basis for the entire structure. Without a strong foundation—and a lot of stability—the first big storm will knock your house down. Having a stable base is vital in a home, a relationship, and a business. In fact, it might even be the most important factor.

> Houses and relationships need a strong foundation to prevent them from crumbling in the long run.

Why? Because the stability of any relationship or business determines what happens next. Think about it. If your relationship is unstable—meaning you can't count on your partner to be there when you need him/her, or they lie all the time, or they walk away when you need emotional support—the relationship will crumble. You can keep trying to patch it up, but you're eventually going to realize you are the only one holding the two halves together, and that's not sustainable.

FIND A STRONG EXAMPLE

When I first started in this industry, I was eighteen and I didn't think about the importance of stability. I owe a lot of the credit to Joe Stumpf, my mentor of over twenty years, who helped me develop a foundational thought process. He was the leader of a coaching company for real estate and mortgage professionals and he gave me a lot of advice that I still use to this day.

I learned early on that the more stable your business is in terms of systems, processes, your team, and customer experience, the longer it will last and the more storms it can easily weather. When you build a house, you don't just say, "Let's skip the trusses and throw the roof on top of the framing," because the entire structure will fall apart. Don't do that in your business, either. Start with stable systems, structured financials, and be accountable to both yourself and your people. As you build those foundations, great customer experiences will grow and become a bigger part of your business.

> Start with having stable systems and financials while being accountable to both yourself and your people.

Michael E. Gerber's book, *The E-Myth,* talks a lot about the importance of not just working *in* your business, but also *on* your business and then being *outside* of your business so you can see all aspects of the company. Every business owner needs to do those three things because that gives them an opportunity to see what's not performing at its best (what isn't stable, in other words) and improve on the models and systems. Engineers, for example, spend a lot of time thinking about how to construct something. They consider the long-term plan of a building, as well as what was already there in the past. They lean on their education and their past experiences to come up with the best possible solution.

CREATE A DEPENDABLE CUSTOMER EXPERIENCE

The key to a great customer experience is taking the time to dive into everything that happens for the customer when they work with your business. You have to take a step back and see their point of view to ensure you are delivering a consistently amazing experience.

It's also important to set expectations early on. We have a consultation with every single customer before we start working with them because it helps both sides to set crystal clear expectations. In this meeting, a couple of things are happening—we let the customers get to know us and tell them what they can expect when they work with us. When we take the time to get to know them, we learn how to anticipate their needs. We discover why they are buying or selling, what things are important to them, and find out what they need most from our company. That allows us to give them what they need before they realize they need it or even ask for it, instead of leaving them to wonder what will happen next.

> ## Set clear expectations early on.

That view from ten thousand feet above the process is vital to customers. Often, buying or selling a house is something they will do a handful of times over the course of their lifetime. It's a big deal and one where they may have dozens of questions. We try to anticipate those questions early on so that the entire transaction is off to a great start.

REGULATE YOUR BUSINESS SYSTEMS

There are certain tasks that every business owner will perform over and over again, whether it's payroll, bookkeeping, or end-of-day reports. If you can take a step back and build a checklist for your systems, it gives the entire team a consistent picture of how your company works.

It also gives you a picture of where you spend the majority of your time. Are your hours better served in sales or marketing? If so, then hire an expert to take on those other systems.

In my marriage, my husband and I balance each other well. Each of us has strengths that the other doesn't. He's completely different from me and our combined abilities help to stabilize our marital team. When I think about long-term relationships, like my grandparents' fifty-year marriage, I've realized that the two people are opposites who balance each other most of the time.

MAINTAIN SOLID LEADERSHIP

This was something that took me a long time to learn. I always thought a leader was the one in charge who made all the decisions but, as I got older and started to emulate and model people I respected, I realized a leader isn't a dictator— it's someone people naturally follow because they are smart, trustworthy, dependable, and genuinely care about their people.

Good leaders don't have to push people to follow them. They don't have to rule with an iron fist. They are the kind of people others naturally gravitate toward because they are leading the entire team in a direction that's good for everyone. It's a win-win, not just a win for one person.

> Good leaders don't have to push people to follow them.

Think of leadership like a relationship. The best leaders bring in people who counterbalance their weaknesses. They have people who provide stability, the capital, or possibly the nurturing piece—there's even a role where a person may be known as the "nervous squirrel" who exercises lots of caution, something that should be seen as a positive quality. If the investor, or the "High C" person (meaning a person who is super analytical and likes a lot of details, spreadsheets, or numbers), in the company sees the glass as half empty, that's okay because some other key player in the company will be the one who sees it as half full. It's the ability to have others around to ask profound questions and even poke holes in the perfect plan. It allows you to see your blind spots. The most important thing is that the whole team is on the same road and collectively they realize that each person's piece of the puzzle will be totally different. Not everyone can be an end piece. Someone has to be the middle. Those middle pieces create the beauty for the end result. As a whole, all of the pieces will build the entire puzzle and the puzzle pieces are the ones that can help you build the foundation of a great company.

HAVE CONSISTENT ACCOUNTABILITY

In *QbQ: The Question Behind the Question* by John G. Miller, he says you can't play the blame game. You have to look at the root cause of whatever is happening. That helps you be accountable to yourself, your team, and for your team to be accountable to you and to each other.

Accountability is crucial for the stability of a company. You have to know that the people you have hired know what is expected of them and are going to do what they say they are going to do. They *will* make mistakes, it's whether or not they take accountability for them and learn from them that's important. It's been challenging at times to hold my people accountable. I try to make sure that I'm very clear as to what their role is and what I expect from them. It's like dating someone who is perpetually late—that disappointment will lead to resentment and eventually could lead to the destruction of the relationship.

It's just as key to hold yourself accountable. If you say, *I'm going to take the trash out*, but you never do it, you send the message that people can't depend upon you.

> Accountability builds trust and no relationship, whether it's personal or business, can last without trust.

That all goes back to setting those expectations early on. I ask my customers in that first meeting what they expect of me and my team. Many times, they have said, "I know that you're going to tell me the truth and that you'll make sure I'm not making a bad decision."

We also get the response "communication" very often as an expectation. If we don't communicate the way they have told us they prefer and with the frequency in which they want it, or if someone on my team fails the customer, then the entire team has failed that person.

People want stability, consistency, and lots of great communication, especially with something as big as a home purchase or a home sale. For example, if you promise to call the customer with an update or a recommendation for a painter, or whatever you've promised, then be sure you call them or do whatever it is that you said you would do. Even with the little things, the customer needs to know they can count on you.

KEYS TO SUCCESS

If you want to create stability for yourself and your business, do this:

1. Start with a strong foundation
2. Find a good example to follow—you can even get a stability mentor
3. Create a customer experience from their point of view
4. Cultivate leadership skills. Take care of your people so they will follow you and your vision with passion
5. Hold yourself and your team accountable
6. Keep your finances in order

7. Watch every dollar and save 15% of your income for wealth building!

HAVE A STABLE FINANCIAL BASE

What does that mean, anyway? I think of money. When one thinks about money, it's all about perspective. My philosophy is that money is good for the good that it can do. Yet without it, it's hard to make the world go 'round. Without it, you can't grow, thrive, or gain leverage to help you. Too little money leads to a scarcity mindset, and a lack of working capital could easily be a source of arguments and stress or the inability to even operate from day to day.

Many, many business owners found this out the hard way when the coronavirus shutdowns hobbled their companies—for months. Smart business owners make sure to watch their money from the beginning. Even if you are a startup and still bootstrapping it, make sure to save money and have some reserves. I like to err on the side of caution and make sure there's enough in reserves to last six months, especially if you are in an industry with flexible or variable income streams.

> Smart business owners make sure to keep an eye on their money from the get-go.

If you don't have that savings in place, then ask yourself if you are truly being accountable for your finances. Are you regularly looking at your expenses? Are you cutting things that aren't serving your customers well? Think those things through before you spend money that might be better served sitting in reserve or used elsewhere.

When we first got married, my husband and I were both irresponsible with money. Our bank account was a train wreck. Neither one of us was really watching the spending or the bank balance, and that was not only stupid, but irresponsible. We had to learn to budget and have the hard conversations most people prefer to avoid—the ones about money—and take a long, hard look at where our money was going.

If you're spending the money in one area, what are you *not* spending it on? Know where your money will go before you ever spend a dime. Have very clear expectations for those hard-earned dollars and the return on their investment. Yes, *investment.* When you go to work in your younger years, you are trading time for money. You must be smart about this because you'll want to trade money for time later on, so you need to have enough of it. It's the difference between being able to retire at any age and not having a choice of retirement and needing to work into your seventies and even eighties versus doing what you want to do with your time.

The simplest advice I ever got was to set aside 15% of all monies earned and sink it into some kind of investment, whether that's simply starting with a separate savings, a retirement account, buying a house, etc.—the point is, ***this money is separate and only for building wealth***. Any money spent should be an investment into something that will make you more money.

A *Bankrate* survey asked a thousand working American adults how much of their annual income they set aside for retirement, emergencies, and other financial goals, only to discover that those who do save weren't setting aside much. Twenty percent replied they save only 5% *or less* of what they make, and 28% save 6 to 10%. Just 16% are saving more than 15 percent of their income. Astonishingly, over 21% of people save nothing.

Most of the American population do not save 15% for wealth building and retirement. So, it's understandable that people are scared about running out of money and why an event like a job loss, a stock market crash, or even a pandemic, can quickly wipe many people out. You're never stuck if you have that reserve fund and you live below your means because that savings gives you choices.

Save 15% of everything you earn.

One of our clients, a young couple with two kids, were relocating to Tampa and buying their first house in the area. They were unfamiliar with the area and afraid of what could go wrong in the process. During our consultation, I found out what was most important to them—schools, community, and dependability for their children. It wasn't about price; it was about the long-term picture of what this home would bring to their family—stability. People crave stability because it gives them a firm place to stand and then grow from. If your relationships and your business are stable, you don't have to worry about them falling apart with the slightest stressor. You can concentrate on making them even stronger.

CHAPTER FIVE
MAKING THE COMMITMENT

COMMITMENT ISSUES.

If there was ever a hot-button topic in relationships, it's the word *commitment*. Making a commitment to another person is when we feel our most vulnerable or scared, and sometimes it makes people feel trapped. Commitment is about a lot more than a ring and a date—it's about trust, something that can be just as difficult to develop in business relationships as it is in personal ones.

There is *always* a reason that people don't commit and it's usually because there is a lack of trust. This is true with any relationship, business or personal. In business, the reason people don't commit is because there is a lack of trust somewhere. The bigger the purchase and the more money involved, the more work you will have to do to bridge the trust gap.

> In business, people don't commit because there is a lack of trust somewhere.

KEYS TO SUCCESS

Gaining trust with clients is a process, comprised of several parts:

1. Honesty and Transparency
2. Follow-Through
3. Keeping Promises
4. Exceeding Expectations
5. Listening, Listening, Listening

When I work with a buyer or seller, it's really important that we have a commitment right from the beginning. After we have engaged thoroughly with clients to discover what they are after and then lay out the plan as to how we will make it happen, the client then agrees to hire me with a listing agreement or buyers' agent agreement. We wouldn't gain their trust without first taking the time to fully understand their perspective and needs, not to mention there would be no agreement.

Often, if there is hesitation or a reservation with a buyer or seller, it's simply because there are still unanswered questions, objections I haven't answered, or I have somehow failed to gain their trust. It's never about money. People simply don't want to feel stuck or trapped. This would be true of any relationship. It's why prenups are signed because there is hesitation somewhere and a small gap where there is a trust missing factor. A prenup covers the "what if I forgot about this" gap.

For something like real estate, what most people don't realize is that a real estate agent, a good one anyway, takes a far greater risk in signing the deal than the prospective client does. An agent takes all of the risk, spends all of the time, money and marketing efforts required to sell the home at a price that is acceptable to you. So when (and if) the agent brings you a qualified buyer that can (and does) close at the agreed upon price, then—and *only then*—do they get paid for the services rendered and get the commission they have earned. Until then, they get nothing—no guarantees and no money, just the opportunity to sell a product and earn the client's trust along the way.

For all of our agreements, our brokerage has a built-in cancellation fee. In most brokerages, this is left completely to the agent's discretion as to whether or not it will be enforced upon the termination of a contract. So, my clients always sign agreements with me where it's built in trust. For example, if they change their minds and decide not to sell, they can still cancel and I waive the termination fee. I had all of the expenses and risk, so it's a business loss for me at this point; but it's more about the trust I earned from my client because I did what I said I would.

Are your clients having commitment issues with you or your team? If so, take a hard look at your team and your process so you discover why and then figure out what you intend to do about it. I assure you there is a reason. Is there a problem with your process? If so, fix it. Is it a problem with your team or a specific member of your team? How committed are they, long term? Believe me, people can feel that.

> There is no commitment without trust.

ARE BOTH PARTIES TRULY READY?

In my industry, I see too many eager agents who jump in and work with people without first securing a commitment, especially on the buyer side. The agents don't take the time to talk about the buyer agreement, asking for a commitment and getting it signed, because they're rushing to get the sale. This representation agreement protects the agent's hard work and time put into helping a buyer find a home, so it's important to take a breath before leaping into a home search with a customer. There are countless hours invested in setting up appointments, finding homes that are good matches, and guiding the buyer through all of the nuisances, potential issues or things that need to happen, gathering information needed to give to the buyer, as well as pairing buyers with great lenders and other service professionals they will need for a successful, smooth transaction—and, trust me, there are many.

It only makes sense to have the agreement in place, but greener agents don't like to have that conversation. Maybe they're not confident enough or they lack the necessary skill and knowledge—but, whatever reason, they aren't having those conversations, which can hurt their bottom line. Real estate agents don't get paid until they help someone buy or sell their home. All those hours and dollars invested upfront aren't recouped until after the sale closes. If you're a buyer's agent and your buyers aren't committing to you, it's going to affect your income. Qualified and really experienced, seasoned agents—like me—know the answers to all of your questions. I only have so many hours in a day, so I won't waste my time with a client who won't commit. I have to spend my time with the ones who do. The fact is that hiring me will keep you out of trouble and save you from the alternative: Having to defend yourself legally because you chose to use an inexperienced agent.

> **I only commit to clients who are willing and ready to commit to me.**

As a real estate agent, you want buyers who are qualified and ready to work with only you. Otherwise, you could end up wasting weeks or months showing them homes they aren't ready or qualified to buy, and you risk losing them to another agent because they didn't call you first. How do you build that readiness between you and your customer?

DEMONSTRATE YOUR VALUE:

Customers like to know that they are with someone who is experienced and who has their best interests at heart. Take the time to discuss your experience and how you will exceed the customer's expectations. A lot of buyers think they don't need an agent. And they don't, *until they do* because the transaction often gets complicated. Sometimes, a complicated transaction requires an attorney to fix a mess they've accidentally created by not leaning on a qualified seasoned professional that could explain the value they bring and help the consumer see what's missing without them.

BE DEPENDABLE:

If things go south, are you there for your customer? Are you answering the phone and solving problems? Can they count on you no matter what happens? Dependability is everything. It's like leaning against a solid pillar of concrete versus a termite-infested, rotten, piece of wood.

BE CONFIDENT:

Be ready to tackle the problems and do so with self-assurance. We once sold a home that was listed as being connected to public utilities. It wasn't; it had a septic tank instead of sewage connections to the city. My buyer talked about suing both the seller and the listing agent. I had to step in and bring some calm to the situation, then pick up the phone and talk to the other agent about a way to solve the problem. It helped that I knew the other agent and that we already had a working relationship. We had the septic tank inspected at no cost to the buyer, which gave the buyer confidence in the home, and saved hours of aggravation and costly attorney fees on a situation that could not be changed after the fact. Had I buried my head in the sand, nothing would have worked out and, in the end, no one would have been happy.

THE PAST DOESN'T ALWAYS PREDICT THE FUTURE

I originally went into real estate because I had a negative experience when I bought my house and I wanted to make sure none of my customers went through the same thing. I've met several customers who had been burned before and they were reluctant to trust another agent. It's up to you to create a fantastic experience and to demonstrate that you are as committed to the relationship as you expect and want the customer to be.

Think about other businesses that you interact with. Apple, for instance, delivers a certain consistent, customer experience. They have built a massive global business because they know the minute they fail to deliver on those expectations is the minute they lose a customer. Reliable, consistent, superior service is far more valuable and reassuring to the customer than telling them over and over again how great you are.

> Be consistent in your customer experience. Your claims of a positive customer experience shouldn't be just lip service— it requires action.

You don't want to just build your customer base—you want to create raving fans, people who will come back to you over and over again and tell everyone they know how well you treated them, as well as how amazing you and your business have been. They will defend your product or service like it was their own. Have you ever heard, or perhaps or even had, a debate over Apple vs. Android? You want your customers to be staunch defenders of your product like folks are when discussing whether the Android phone is better than the latest iPhone.

People who are afraid of committing are often afraid of being burned again. They don't trust others and they definitely don't feel comfortable handing over control or sharing the driver's seat with someone else. Buying a home is a huge commitment and it's up to you, as the agent representing their best interests, to help them understand what they are signing up for financially as well as the rewards they can reap by building equity and wealth in their real estate transactions.

> It is up to you to help your customers understand the gravity of their commitment.

We talk to our customers about everything from wire fraud to additions made without a permit and how it can impact them. We talk to them about what can go wrong, and how we can navigate around these major things. We stress over and over again that we are all in this together, and that we will always have a Plan B if things go wrong. *Always.*

You need to set the expectations for what will happen next and keep surprises, if there are any, at bay. People get scared when they don't know what to expect and many sales have been lost because the agent was unable to manage client expectations and keep unwanted surprises to a minimum.

After the coronavirus pandemic, these open conversations became even more important. Asking what the buyer did for a living was just as important as asking if they were qualified to buy. Is there a chance their job will be furloughed? In the market crash of 2008, we saw dozens of pending sales fall apart. Your customer doesn't want that to happen and neither do you, so do the research that keeps the ship from potentially sinking. As Gary Keller said in the book *Shift*, it's about bulletproofing the transaction.

Any great company has two things at the forefront: Knowing their customers inside and out and being super committed to them. That breeds loyalty which, in turn, encourages you and the company to go the extra mile. It's a win-win for everyone and good for the long-term health of your business.

STOP LOOKING FOR GREENER GRASS

I've been married for twenty-five years and people ask me all the time how my husband and I make a long-term relationship work. I think one of the keys to a strong commitment is keeping your focus on your own lawn instead of looking over the fence at what might seem like greener grass.

> The grass isn't always greener on the other side of the fence. Water your own lawn.

When we first got married, we had no idea how much we would each change and grow over the course of more than two decades. It's a choice to continue being committed to each other and to the relationship itself. Of course, no one's goal when they get married is to get divorced. Avoiding a breakup and maintaining that commitment over the long haul is about having common goals both of you work toward, as well as checking in with your partner about what is important to them, how they are feeling, and what concerns they have.

The exact same principles apply for maintaining long-term customer relationships. You have to listen, be on the same page, and not push your customer into a bad decision. For example, if someone says they want to look at homes under $300,000, I'm not doing them any favors by showing them houses they can't afford at $350,000. Staying within their expectations and showing that I have a genuine interest in working within those parameters helps build that trust between us.

If the agent has open lines of communication with the customer about why things should happen a certain way, like you're recommending that they price the home at a certain dollar amount, why you recommend home staging, or why you want to host a showing at a particular time, then the customer will develop trust and can relax into the relationship with you. In addition, having sympathy for things like the difficulties of living in a staged home when a customer has three kids all under the age of ten or is helping care for an elderly parent, means offering solutions that minimize the impact on the sellers. When the customer feels left out of the loop or misunderstood, they get scared and often go looking for another solution or person to work with. Avoid this by not just communicating—but listening, too.

BUILDING LONG-TERM SUCCESS

Being committed to your customers—and finding customers who are committed to you—are crucial elements for the long-term success of your business. If you're not building lasting relationships, then it's time to take a step back, evaluate, and ask some hard questions.

Is your competition delivering something you aren't?

Are they finding properties that aren't on the open market?

Do they work well with other agents?

Are they doing what it takes to make their listing stand out in a crowded marketplace?

The best agents set their customers up to succeed, not just today but way into the future. They guide them through the best financial decisions, give them options for reducing debt, and help them to create wealth for tomorrow. I want every one of my clients to succeed—and I want them to stay with me as customers for life and be the kind of customer that tells everyone about me and my product or service.

Making that happen starts with my commitment to them and to put my best foot forward with every single transaction and conversation. That's the way to have a business with staying power. I have grown with many of my customers, personally and professionally. I earned that relationship by helping them in ways that others could not or did not.

> You want customers for life, don't you?

CHAPTER SIX
BREAKUPS

Everything is going along great, everyone seems happy, and the days ahead look bright and sunny; at least, that is the way one party felt. The other party may be thinking, "How the heck do I get out of this?" or maybe they're just not *feeling* the relationship anymore. Then, seemingly without warning, the relationship is over, they've unlinked their social media accounts, or maybe they just disappeared leaving the other party struggling to figure out what went wrong. A breakup, whether it's personal or business, is always pretty traumatic and can leave you wondering, "What the heck just happened!?"

FIGURE OUT THE WHY

The first thoughts a business owner should have are: Why are we breaking up? Why are they firing me? Why are they returning my product? Why are they no longer doing business with my company? Why is this conversation happening? It may not save *that* customer but knowing the why is critical to making changes that avoid another breakup or loss of a customer.

No matter why a customer is leaving your business, the breakup always hurts. However, there is always a way to learn and grow and to become better at what you do. In The book *QBQ!* by John Miller, he says to ask yourself, "The question behind the Question". In other words, use self-accountability and leave the victim mentality behind. You can't change other people so change your own thinking.

A question I might ask myself would be, "What can I do differently that would give me a different outcome?" If a client is firing me, I'm not afraid to ask them what went wrong and if there is something I can fix or correct. If you don't ask the question, you won't learn the reasons and you won't improve. Everyone can learn something to be a better businessperson, regardless of your industry or how many years you have invested. Simply ask yourself better open-ended questions to expose the roots.

> If you don't ask the questions,
> you don't learn the reasons and you won't improve.

There are also questions to be asked on the opposite side of the breakup. If you're the one firing the customer, so to speak, what learning lesson should you take from that? Is there a red flag you missed in the beginning? Did you try to work with customers who didn't fit your ideal business demographic? What questions should you have asked in the beginning to discover if you were a match?

If I take on a customer knowing they weren't a good match, then that's on me; especially if I'm not asking the important questions. For instance, I have a number of clients who come to me to sell their property because of a divorce, overextension of debt, probate, or other court order. It's up to me to ask them profound questions to get to their why behind selling. Not just the life event that's precipitating the sale, but why am I here to begin with? How long have you been thinking about selling? What's driving that choice right now? Who gets the proceeds from this sale? Does everyone (all the owners) want to sell? What amount do you need to net in this sale? What's important about that? Where will you go when we sell this home? Are there any other contingencies involved?

There's a reason someone is hiring me to sell the home to begin with, and once I meet with them it's my job to take a deep dive into why I'm *really* there so I can see it from their perspective and craft a very specific and strategic plan around their needs. Let's face it, no one wakes up and says "I want to sell my home, so I think I'll call a Realtor® today". They have been thinking about it for weeks, or even months, and those seeds are planted because of very specific events or driving factors that continue to drive the thoughts and conversations in their head.

> To start to understand the 'break up'
> with a customer, start by asking why.
> And then dig deeper.

It's the same thing when a relationship ends. Most of us ask why, but are we diving deep enough to figure out the reasons *behind* the why? Was there a connection you missed? A need you didn't meet for your partner? An expectation that wasn't fulfilled? Are you accepting your part in what you could have changed?

IT'S NOT ME, IT'S YOU

When a breakup happens, it's always easier to blame the other person rather than take personal accountability, right? The same is true in business. It's easier to blame the client or say their expectations were too high or that they were too demanding. Too many business owners never take responsibility for what happens or, worse, they didn't even notice the customer was gone and failed to stop and think about what really happened. The truth is. It's rarely only one person's fault. You have to look at yourself as much as you do the other party.

> All of life is for learning.

I'm a lifelong learner. I'll never be at a place where I think I have all the answers and can't improve. That will never happen. Some of the smartest people I know realize that there is always so much more to learn. The more you know, the more you realize how much you really don't know. My approach is to do a regular check-in with my staff and my customers to make sure I'm still delivering an amazing experience, and we are all on the same page.

If I let that get away from me, it wouldn't take long for the entire business to turn upside down. Think about it, some of the best restaurants will always have a manager pop by your table to make sure that everything is perfect. Ever wonder why? Simply because great restaurants know that people like me, won't complain, *we just won't come back.* But if someone were to ask me point blank, "What was the best part of your experience today?" They would discover what was amazing or if something wasn't. You don't want to do this when it's too late! It's never too early to ask how things are going.

> The more you know, the more you realize how much you really don't know.

THE BLESSING IN THE BREAKUP

To me, insight is God's whisper of direction. He's nudging you down the right path—but it's up to you to listen and learn. If you aren't doing that, you're missing out on great conversations with yourself. Always look for the insight in every day and in every life experience. I assure you, it's there. You just have to look for it.

The pandemic of 2020 wasn't a breakup but it did cause a break in business for most of the world. It was definitely not business as usual for anyone. I could have looked at that as a negative but, instead, I chose to look for the positive. To me, it was God's way of hitting the reset button on our lives. A message telling us all to take some time to slow down and think about what is most important to us. Life is so busy and moves so fast that most people just seemed more irritated by the slowdown than using it as an opportunity to look for the blessing.

One day, my husband told me that one of his employees once said, "There's prejudice everywhere; you just have to look for it." He was so taken aback by this comment. My immediate thought was that people always find what they are looking for, which applies to everyone and to pretty much everything. You will find what you're looking for, good or bad. If you keep looking for negatives that's all you're going to see. But the reverse is also true—if you are constantly searching for upsides, insights and lessons, you'll find exactly what you are searching for. The lesson here? *Be aware of what you are seeking, you will find it.* Sound familiar? Matthew 7:7 says, "… seek, and ye shall find; knock, and it shall be opened to you…"

We're all human and we all make mistakes. By taking a step back and trying to see the other person's perspective, you can sometimes repair or alleviate a breakup altogether. Sure, there are some people who complain about their steak because they want a free meal, but in my experience that's a rare occasion. Sometimes the customer just needs to feel that they are heard, they are important, and their business is valued.

Experience gives you a certain amount of insight, partly because you have more years in the business and partly because you have more years of life experience. People who get married in their twenties often don't have the life experience and relationship experience to understand their spouse. They sometimes react faster and walk away easier, simply because they haven't had years of experience to work problems out. When it gets to that point, you have a choice in the relationship—to call it quits or to do things differently a different future can be created. Can I take responsibility for my actions and reactions? What can I change or not change? Those words turn into your thoughts and your thoughts turn into your actions, and those all lead to change.

> Don't lose the lesson as you gain experience.

When your customer comes to you with a complaint, be sure to take the time to thank them for sharing their perspective with you and allowing them to be honest and transparent about their issues. Then ask for the opportunity to fix whatever went wrong. Lots of customer relationships can be salvaged just by asking if you can make it right. Afterwards, take the time to figure out what could have gone better and what you can change.

BE SURE IT'S NOT THE WHO

I had a very dear client, a young family that had gone through several transactions with us as their family grew—a townhome, a starter home, and then a bigger house. The last time we talked, however, she said, "We almost didn't come back to work with your company again." I asked her to tell me more about that and, as we talked, I discovered that I had the wrong Who in my business: they had problems with someone on my team that they worked with in a previous transaction. I made a bad hire. The personalities sometimes didn't mesh well, so their experience wasn't as good as it could have been.

Before a relationship is dismantled and a valuable customer is lost, take a look at the Who and make sure you have the right pairing between customer and staff. You also have to check on the experience with your customers. Ask them early and often to head problems off at the pass or it may be too late.

The Who is everything, really. Think about it this way—if you were to sit down as a single person and make a list of what you want in a great partner, you'll be able to narrow down the Who. Someone who's physically active maybe, or someone who likes to travel? A person who is vegan or one who loves dogs? Whatever your parameters, knowing them and then speaking them aloud helps you to ultimately find that person. That's the concept behind the law of attraction and changing your thoughts, as well as affirmations with books like *The Secret*. Pay attention to the people around you because if you aren't pairing yourself—or your customers—with the right Who, things can easily go south.

It's often difficult to find the right employees because many people hire out of necessity. Often, there's a pain point or a gap they are trying to fill and know hiring a warm body will be okay in the short-term rather than strategizing their hires to maximize their plan for the long run.

KEYS TO SUCCESS

Hiring the right people builds a better foundation for the company as a whole, and a strong foundation creates a stable business. Ask the right questions from the start.

- What is your customer service philosophy?
- Why are you in this industry?
- How do you handle setbacks?
- What makes you different from other people with a similar product or service?

We've changed our hiring process over the years. We are constantly looking for great talent for our organization but every hire starts with a meet and greet to let people get to know me and my team. During that time, we share who we are, what makes us different, what we are and are not, and we are very real with them about what the real estate business is like.

We give potential employees a personality assessment and follow models of a detailed hiring process I learned at Keller Williams Realty. This process digs deep into who they are, how they think, and gives the company some insight on how the hirees will naturally operate and how they might respond under pressure.

We've learned to be slow to hire and quick to fire when either side isn't serving the other well. If our organization isn't a match for them, we want to set them free or maybe even help place them with a more suitable organization or into a different role where they can be happy and thrive.

It also works in reverse. If you've had a breakup, I would encourage anyone listening to or reading this book to think about what went wrong, what you wanted, and what your ideal outcome would have been. Ask amazing questions that begin with "what," and deep dive into them. Describe those concepts in detail. It's easy to list everything that's wrong—but what's the flip side? What are the things that went right? What are the things that could benefit you and your business or relationships? When you get really granular on all those statements about what you are looking for with the time frame and specificity, you see that it's actually achievable. It creates a list, or a roadmap of sorts, to get from where you are to where you want to be.

> Consider the attraction factor, that's where it all starts.

The more granular you are in that plan and process, the more of a reality that picture becomes for you. The truth is that anyone can become a millionaire, have a great relationship, or run a great business. However, you don't go from zero to hero without a lot of experience, reaching milestones, and learning many lessons along the way.

Life has a way of preparing you for where you are going and where you want to be. If you don't have certain experiences, you can't get to where you want to go. So, welcome those experiences and wrong turns—they can become a blessing that leads to the next great destination!

> See your experiences and wrong turns as preparation for where you want to be, not what's holding you back.

A breakup feels a lot like a failure. However, many of the greatest minds of our time failed over and over again. Henry Ford went broke many times and even filed for bankruptcy twice before he succeeded. What if he had given up? Where would the automobile industry be today?

I pay attention to companies that have done what I want to do and then model them to get what I am trying to achieve. It makes sense, right? If you want to be married for fifty years, you ask people who have been married for five decades for relationship advice, not the friend who is getting divorced for the third time. If you want to be a millionaire, talk to millionaires for advice, not your broke uncle. If you want to have a great company, look at other great companies and discover how they got to where they are.

Southwest Airlines revolutionized flying by making it into a fun experience, changing all of the status quo rules and identifying who their customer was, as well as who their competition was and wasn't. Surprisingly, it was not other airlines, it was the automobile. One of the most profitable moments for Herb Kelleher was when he realized their planes don't make any money on the ground. He made it clear to everyone on the Southwest Airlines team that the only time the company is making money is when their planes are in the air.

Their employees understood this at a high level, so they made the flying experience as different and as amazing as possible. This approach inspired operational efficiencies and encouraged customers to choose Southwest Airlines over other traditional airline options. They found inefficiencies and changed the way people were boarding the plane, ticketing, interactions with customers and more. They were competing against all forms of transportation, not just airlines, so Kelleher knew they had to go above and beyond in order to make a profit. Herb Kelleher died January 3, 2019 but his leadership, profits, and culture will forever be his legacy.

If a breakup happens, try not to let it shake your confidence. Sure, you might have made some mistakes, but that doesn't mean you can't take some lessons and make some changes in the future. Everything in business—good and bad—is a learning experience and you are going to pay for that education, one way or another.

> **Smart millionaires earn as they learn.**

Final thought, if something is broken, don't just look for ways to change things and make them better—revolutionize the way things are done. Don't let anyone tell you that you can't, because you could be the next Henry Ford, Herb Kelleher, or Elon Musk if you put your mind to it.

CHAPTER SEVEN
REBOUNDS

I think we've all been there—you fall in love, the relationship ends, and you're heartbroken. Then wham! You meet someone else to get over the pain and fill the void and you're instantly in love. That new love fizzles out pretty quickly, though, and you realize it was just a rebound. Sort of like boomeranging your feelings onto someone else.

I think it's human nature to want to fill the hole in your life, but I would encourage you to think about WHY before you make any decisions. Why are you in this situation right now? Why didn't it work out with the last customer or company? Why are you talking to this new one? Where are your shortcomings?

DON'T RUSH ANYTHING

Going into a relationship too quickly after one is broken can be like pulling a rubber band back too far. The harder and farther you pull, the bigger the snap will be and more it will hurt when it breaks! Too many of us rush from one situation to the next. We're too focused on filling that gap that we make decisions without thinking it through. Let's take a couple sample scenarios and play it through.

> Take your time. Reflect. Then act to attract your next opportunity or relationship.

A long-time customer jumps ship and starts working with your competitor. Without a word. You're definitely bound to be hurt and upset. You run right out and land another customer in that same demographic and think you have fixed the problem. But have you?

Why did the original customer leave? Are those problems still there? If so, the next customer will also leave. The same red flags that ended the first relationship will tank the second one before it ever gets off the ground because you haven't done the work to set things right. Like we talked about in the last chapter, it's important to know *why* a customer leaves. Ask these questions when the *first* customer leaves, not the hundredth. Don't rush to fill the gap left behind—find out why the gap exists at all.

Being prepared keeps you from rushing into bad business decisions, too. Maybe you lose a third of your business in a month and you then hastily sign a partner to work with you. Months later, that partnership is soured but the two of you are financially tangled, so it won't be easy to dismantle the deal.

KEYS TO SUCCESS

Always have a plan. I know that sounds fundamental, but you'd be surprised how many people don't have a strategic plan for their lives, their relationships, or their business. Once you create a plan, it naturally builds steps and decisions to make in order to achieve your goal.

The housing crash of 2008 is a prime example. It not only destroyed the real estate markets, it also affected things globally. For four months, I went to work every single day without a paycheck but I still paid all my bills. How? By saving, I was prepared for that eventuality: The crash we already knew was coming someday.

Most people, including most of the American population, can't even make it one or two weeks without a paycheck, let alone one month or more. Imagine showing up at your job, day in and day out, without a guaranteed paycheck. Sure every business needs revenue, but with sustained savings you can prepare for the unknown. If you can't see yourself surviving financially, then it's time to make some smarter financial decisions for your company and yourself.

One of the biggest lessons that I learned from 2008 was to be very wise about any decision I make regarding money and to always have enough savings to make it through the next financial crisis (like the 2020 pandemic). That means living far below my means and not driving a brand-new car. In the end, though, does it really matter what the neighbors think about your house or your car? You're focusing on what's important to you—stability, both personally and professionally, so you can be there to serve the next customer or launch the next business venture. Be ready for opportunities others can't take advantage of. I'm not going to be in a position where I have to rush out and fill a hole just for the sake of filling it.

> Be ready and prepare for the unexpected, otherwise you will make decisions out of desperation. Those decisions will only hurt you and cost you more in the long run.

Financial security buys me time to think through my decisions. It keeps me from being pressured into jumping in on the next hot thing, as that bandwagon may be a huge misstep. I can sit back, look at what went wrong, really think through a solid plan, and regroup before moving into another lane.

As many of my great mentors have said over the years, "If you fail to plan, just plan to fail." This is true with everything in life from parenting, to business, to marriages. The more detailed the plan, the more executable it is and the less chance there is of failure.

Think about this, just in terms of your life partner. When you want to plan a great evening out, you spend time thinking about what you both would enjoy, where you want to go, what you're going to wear, whether you need a babysitter, etc. There are so many details to cover in planning a simple evening out. Why not do the same for your business or your finances?

> Have a financial plan.
> A relationship plan.
> A business plan.

DON'T SEE WITH ROSE-COLORED GLASSES

Some people are so burned by a bad experience or feel so jaded that they avoid making any decisions at all. Some people return to a bad situation because they don't like change and just want to stay with what's familiar. They don't even look at other options, even though they know they could have a better experience elsewhere. They look past the negatives just so they don't have to make a change.

The flip side is true, too—if you work with someone amazing, you might not realize how incredible they are and take them for granted. That happens all the time in relationships. You hear people say, "I didn't know what I had until it was gone," or "I thought the grass was greener elsewhere."

The truth is the grass isn't always greener. Sometimes the grass is barely being maintained. It just has a great façade. I look at my clients as friends and I try to keep it all in perspective when things have gone wrong between us. All relationships hit impasses or have things that blow up. Take a breath and maybe chalk it up to someone having a bad day or had too much to drink at a party. One misstep can be overlooked but pay attention if it becomes a pattern.

> Don't let go of a relationship that took
> years to build over one bad moment.
> As I've mentioned before: Communicate.

Always try to see things from the other person's perspective, too. That's true in long-term relationships and also in business connections. When someone is getting heated, I literally take a moment, and then pause and breathe rather than adding more gasoline to the fire—which I did plenty of in my younger years. It's better to leave it alone, walk away, and come back later when you have a chance to think things through and to see things more clearly.

DON'T RUSH THE TIMING

Trust is key to making any kind of relationship work, but trust doesn't happen overnight. Relationships are built over time. My reputation precedes me now because I've been in business so long. But that didn't happen in the beginning. I had to work hard with every single new client and peer to earn that trust and build that relationship.

> Relationships are built over time.
> Have patience with the process.

I had a customer come to me well after the housing market collapsed. He was thinking of buying an investment property, but James had gotten badly burned financially during the crash, and his guard was up. We had many conversations, until he relaxed and realized I was in this for the long haul. When you make a commitment in a real estate transaction but you have no trust foundation, it's like saying you're getting married but you don't trust your spouse.

In his book, *The Speed of Trust*, Stephen M.R. Covey said, "**Trust** always affects two measurable outcomes: **speed** and cost. When **trust** goes down—in a relationship, on a team, in a company, in an industry, with a customer—**speed** decreases with it." In other words, when the trust is there everything is faster, things move along easier and more efficiently. When people enter into a transaction without trust, everything is slower and takes longer—and that's when lawsuits happen.

Any business transaction should start with a consultation and an understanding of what the customer wants at the core level. The only dumb questions are the ones you don't ask. Don't assume you know what a customer is thinking because your assumptions may be very different from their reality. Some of the questions we ask during our consultations are: Why are they selling? Why are they buying? Why are they hesitating to do either? Knowing those answers helps you be their advocate, and allows you to focus and guide them through the perfect plan, not be just another salesperson looking for money from the next deal.

> ## The only dumb questions are the ones you don't ask.

Don't be afraid of awkward silence. I often have to coach my agents through being silent when waiting for answers. When you ask someone a question and they don't know the answer immediately, that's okay. They are searching. Give them space. You've asked them a question that requires some thought, and the biggest mistake you can make is filling that silence with your words just for the sake of talking. **Shut up and let them think!** It will seem like there is awkward silence but, trust me, you are waiting for gold and it's well worth the wait.

Sometimes the question is so deep and requires so much thought that a customer might say things like, "I don't understand what you mean," or ask, "say that again" (this a clue that they aren't fully present, physically and subconsciously). This is when your listening skills get put to the test and you have to realize it's not personal. You need to think and then ask the question again in a way that requires them to listen, which often means repeating their words back to them and rephrasing your query so their response is really what you need to know.

Later, the questions should flow more easily in both directions. Encourage your customers to ask about anything that confuses or scares them. Business people should have the heart of a teacher and answer questions in a way that makes the customer feel confident about the transaction.

Don't be afraid to inject a bit of humor when it's appropriate. Talk about the elephant in the room. Don't ignore it hoping it will go away. For instance, if your home listing is just sitting on the market and we haven't talked about the showings and price, and with feedback about what's going on in the rest of the market, then I'm not serving you at a high level. In short, I'm not doing my job at a high level.

DON'T HIDE THE TRUTH

Technology and the world have changed so much since I have been married. If you've ever looked at a dating app, you'll see pictures that are skating on the edge of being completely fake. People use photos from ten years ago or with a blurred airbrushed Snapchat filter, erasing all those wrinkles and gray roots. It's gotten to the point where you don't even recognize them in person from their online photo. You can't start a relationship based on a lie, and you shouldn't do that in business either. Honesty is the key, even if the conversations are tough ones to have.

For instance, going back to a seller and telling them their price is too high for the market is never a fun conversation. People often have skewed realities when it comes to their own homes. I'm transparent about all of it, from price, to pets, to the smell of smoke or how awful the 1970s wallpaper is that's still in the bathroom of an elite South Tampa neighborhood, I just call it like I see it. I don't deliver unrealistic comparable home sales that don't really compare or give false expectations about pricing, while only preparing to later go in for a price reduction. Many real estate agents, do this, but that's just not how I operate.

I had a customer come to me with a half-million-dollar home that he and his partners insisted was worth $600,000. They were adamant about the price, despite our advice. We did everything we could—staged it twice, had two different photography sessions—and it didn't sell at that price. I had to have a frank conversation with them about the money they would net, the price they would get in the current market, and not be afraid to lose them as clients because of my honesty.

Agents like us have our thumbs on the market's pulse. We have a good idea of what's happening next because we follow the numbers and market trends. When we know we are in a market shift, we plan for that. If we know we are in a trending downward market, we have to get ahead of it. When that happens, we can't price homes out of the range. It will harm our clients more in the end by *not* having those conversations and ultimately net them less money.

In any business, you don't want to sit on inventory you aren't selling, so being aware of the market and what people will pay for products or services helps you get ahead of losses. If you're chasing the market down, you're always going to get less than you would if you had kept the pricing right from the beginning.

If you don't do that, the market will issue its own price correction—and you don't want to be on the losing end of that. Depending on the market, it's okay to test at a higher price initially but be willing to course-correct quickly and get back on track.

My advice is not the same for everyone. It's situational. That's because I know every single customer well and don't just leap from transaction to transaction. My competition isn't Zillow—because my value is about a lot more than a dynamic website and some pricing algorithms. I make sure the customer knows my value from the very beginning, so they don't have a reason to think about going elsewhere. They trust me and know I have their best interests at heart.

> I make sure the customer knows my value from the very beginning, so they don't have a reason to think about going elsewhere.

It takes time to really get to know people personally in order to figure out what makes them tick and to uncover their personality styles. You have to get to know their immediate and extended family. What are some of their long-term goals, and how do you fit into that plan? Do they need an introduction to someone that you can help facilitate? What do they do for work and do they love it? What are their dreams? Where are their social circles? What do they like to do for fun? Are they spiritual? Do they drink? Is it red wine, white wine, beer, or maybe they're a recovering alcoholic?

All of these little pieces fit into the big picture. It's like you're putting together a puzzle and you're slowly sorting through all of the pieces and putting it together to make something beautiful. No matter how fast you want it to be finished, it will take time to do it right.

> You can't force a piece that doesn't fit.

CHAPTER EIGHT
MAKE-UP SEX

Dan and Cheryl have had the same fight a hundred times. It's always about how much money they should be saving instead of spending. At the end of the week, Dan brings home a brand-new Lexus from the local dealership and Cheryl gets mad. They fight, but then Dan ends the argument and they have a little make-up sex. The issue gets tabled and forgotten. For the moment, anyway.

Chances are that Dan and Cheryl will be having this exact same fight about finances again in a few days. And a few days after that. And the next month, and the one after that. Makeup sex is serving as a band-aid for a problem, it's not a solution.

That doesn't just happen in the regular world—making up without solving the problem is also a common tactic in the business world. In business, it's often far too easy to send a customer flowers for a delivery mix-up or write a check for a damaged doorway or give out a free dessert for a delayed entrée. Just like make-up sex, those things are temporary patches that don't really fix anything. If you constantly have to apologize, write a check, or fight a lawsuit on a regular basis, then something deeper is at play.

Look, I get it. Business owners don't like facing angry customers. No one likes to get yelled at or criticized. Sending a dozen roses is a whole lot easier than having that difficult conversation. But before you call FTD, ask yourself: "How often am I making things up to my customers or clients?"

And then ask yourself *Why*. What is the core issue making customers unhappy?

> Get to the root cause of your unhappy customers instead of constantly making up trying to 'fix' the problem.

If you don't know, then take a couple of steps back. Get some feedback and input, even if it's input that hurts your feelings. You're looking to improve, to head off potential disasters, and to show that you are committed to real change and not just real roses. This is where consultants get it, and they have an outside perspective looking in so insight is much easier for them because they aren't attached to anything. They can see all of the holes in your swiss cheese. They can see your blind spots.

DON'T BE DESPERATE

Some businesses go overboard trying to accommodate people, welcome new customers, and even repair customer relationships. A friend of mine went to a new dentist, after seeing an ad in a newspaper with a new customer special. When she showed up for the appointment, she was the only customer there. The entire office came out to greet her, even the dentist. When her cleaning was done, they took a photo of her with the entire office and posted it on social media, welcoming her to the practice. A few days later, she got a card in the mail, gushing about how happy they were to have her in the practice and that they were looking forward to seeing her again.

It was borderline stalking at that point. It screams, "We are not busy and clenching onto every person we can. The overly enthusiastic, overblown reception drove my friend away instead of encouraging her to return. When she didn't make a second appointment, the office made several phone calls and left voicemails asking her why. This was a brand-new potential relationship that the business ruined by being desperate and pushy. Ever had a date like this? Talk about being creeped out and encouraged to run away! The more they push, the more you pull away.

People can feel desperation.

Customers need to feel comfortable and at ease when they talk to you. They want to *feel* like your only customer *(even though they know they aren't)* when you're talking with them, so *be fully present.* The minute they catch that strong scent of desperation it will make them question if you are working with them because you *want* to or because you *have* to.

The biggest complaint I get from my customers is that they want to talk to me more often. Sometimes, they feel they don't get enough of my time. I understand that, but my time is a limited resource. I also know that if they were my *only customer* (and thus I could spend many uninterrupted hours talking to them), they would have a lot more to worry about than whether or not I only have a few minutes for a conversation. This is where trust, experience, and ample time front loaded at the beginning of a relationship come back into play. Even though my time can be limited later, my being fully present and mindful when I am with a new customer— listening intently and giving them my undivided attention in that moment—can make or break everything. This deep intent listening builds the trust needed so that they can lean on me and count on me because I really heard what they said.

Even if your business is in dire straits, don't give off an air of desperation or the perception that you're taking any and every customer who comes your way. Maintain your confidence in every business dealing and make every customer feel like they are unique, special, and working with a powerhouse company.

> You have to genuinely care. You can't teach someone to care about customers. You just do.

DON'T MASK THE PROBLEMS

Make-up sex is often just a cover for the real problems in a relationship. It creates a false sense of joy and security, and it buys a little time until the problem returns. However, recurring problems eventually lead to recurring losses—and who needs that?

If you are doing that in business and burying your head in the sand, ignoring what is going on, and the business choices you are making seem to suck, then you're going to take a huge hit on your bottom line. You can't send enough flowers or free desserts to unsink a ship—you have to figure out what is broken and what's causing the problem to reoccur, and do it fast.

Sometimes, your own ego is the problem. Are you truly the smartest person in the room to deal with this problem? Is there another employee, colleague, or mentor who can take an outside look at the company's issues and offer recommendations? Often, that impartial opinion is the best and truest perspective. Don't ignore it, even if what they are saying hurts. Muscles initially hurt when you stretch them, too.

> Keep working those feedback muscles to make your business stronger.

When I hire people, I look for individuals who hold the same values and believe in the vision and corporate culture I'm constantly creating. I also look for people who have skill sets I don't have. The best way to build a team is to assemble all the structural pieces by bringing in people who have varying strengths. Hiring the right talent from the get-go is one of the most important things you will ever do in business, just as finding the right spouse is the most important decision you'll make for a successful marriage.

FIND FRIENDS WITH BENEFITS

Success is all about the relationships you make and maintain. Being strategic is not just smart, it's necessary. I think back to some of the business relationships I've made in the years since I started my radio show, *Tampa Home Talk*, in 2013. I realize those alliances were exactly what I needed to build my business. The sponsors who wrote those early checks were truly committed to everything we did. They could see the value in me and the value in what we were building. They knew I was in it for the long haul, and they wanted to be part of it.

KEYS TO SUCCESS

It's not all about you. Seriously, it's not. Be a giving person, with no expectations in return, and you will build the kind of relationships you want. Help the neighbor. Recommend the business. Call the friend. Go the extra mile.

The people I align myself and my business with are smart, successful, and become a great extension of myself and our business. For instance, my partner Sarah, my mortgage broker, has been my partner since day one, because I decided to look for someone to replace me when I decided to no longer to write mortgages. Someone who wouldn't grind out mortgage after mortgage but would invest *in relationships* and truly look for solutions to help people. Over the years, I've been able to lean into these amazing relationships I've cultivated over three decades of being in the industry. None of this is just about selling a home—it's about a much bigger picture for me and everyone I align with.

Are the people on your team aligning into your long-term goals, needs, desires and business vision for the future? Or are they just temporary friends with benefits? By anticipating your customers' needs before they come up, you are structuring your business for the long term. If you don't, customers will eventually leave because someone else is going to offer it better, faster or cheaper.

Know who your competition is and what they are delivering. Then strive to do more with less resources, and all while delivering an incredible experience. Have the kind of customer service you would deliver to your mother or brother. You should be treating your customers the way you'd treat a family member. This is where I think most real estate agents miss the mark. They are looking at people as money and just another transaction and not treating every customer as if it's their own child buying their first home or their grandfather looking to fund his retirement in a house sale. Put the customer's needs ahead of your own, and they will sense that you are truly invested in their outcome and overall happiness.

All of that comes back to those questions I asked earlier in the book—*How is your business different from your competition's? Who is your ideal customer? What kind of experience do you want your customer to have in working with you?*

The world is big enough for my business and yours and a thousand others like it. We are each unique individuals, and, because of that, our businesses and our customer relationships will be unique. Figure out those differences and use those to make your business not just good—make it great.

So many of my business relationships have shifted into friendships and we hang out after their transaction is complete. At this stage of my career, I choose the people I work with because I actually like them and that creates a better, happier work environment and work/life balance *for me*. Over time, working with people you don't like has a negative impact on your mental health and, by extension, everything you do personally and professionally. My philosophy is simply this: *If I can't see myself wanting to enjoy having a cup of coffee, beer, or dinner with that person when it's all said and done, then I rethink who I'm getting into a relationship with.*

The alliances I form aren't just about "help me and I'll help you". I want to know how I can help the people who work with me, not vice versa. That stems from maintaining a super servant attitude and always coming from a place of gratitude and an abundance mentality.

We've seen this in action hundreds of times during the Covid-19 pandemic of 2020. Neighbors, businesses, and total strangers banded together for the greater good. No one asked, "What's in it for me?" People have shared everything from toilet paper to helping elderly neighbors by running their errands, and helping communities by supporting local restaurants and businesses.

> Adopt a super servant mentality and be grateful.

One of the things that Dave Ramsey often says is, "When you're on a roller coaster ride, the people who get hurt are the ones who jump off while it's moving." After all, good stewardship starts at the top and works its way down.

Doesn't it? Smart people prepare for economic roller coasters. No one can predict every pandemic or market crash that comes our way.

As a company, our decision in those situations is to have and use our rainy-day reserves. If we deplete those without a course correction and things are still bad economically, we'll lose talent. By strengthening your leaders financially, it could even lead to upper management volunteering to take a pay cut when things are bad. Great leaders are prepared to pivot quickly and we have to lead by example and not by selfishness, desperation, or being destitute.

Our company culture is about helping each other and being upfront and honest. That helps us avoid the necessity of needing an MSR (Making S*it Right) budget to regularly send clients free desserts and floral bouquets. I think so many more relationships and marriages would last twenty times longer if people simply realigned their perspective and realized *we are in this together*. It's an alliance and, when you are in it together, you do the hard work to address the issues and fix the pain points of the current reality.

I think one of the reasons I've been married this long is because my husband is that selfless person who does so much to keep our marriage together. He gets most of the credit for the past two and a half decades we have been together. He's a patient person who has had a totally different perspective on most things. We absolutely balance each other out because we couldn't be more opposite on most things. Part of our success is me being the Ying to his Yang. Over the years, I've learned this: Don't avoid issues—address them and make the necessary changes to redirect your mutual path to success. Do the same with your business and you'll find yourself having a lot more success and happy customers.

We are in this together.

CHAPTER NINE
PRENUPS AND POSTNUPS

No one gets married planning to get divorced. The couple enters the union with the best of intentions, but statistics say that half of those best intentions will end up dissolved by a court. Pre and postnuptial agreements are meant to protect one or both parties' assets, and hopefully avoid a lengthy court battle.

It's a form of preparing for the unthinkable. Most of us don't do that and, when a disaster strikes (like a pandemic that drags on for months and impacts every single business in the world), we aren't ready and we can't pivot fast enough. We're not prepared—and often lose the assets we worked so hard to build.

READ BETWEEN THE LINES

Most realtors use the same state-specific, attorney-approved listing and purchase agreements. Partly because its broker mandated and partly because the standard contract is what customers expect. If you decide to get fancy and write your own, the customers' antenna (or that of the agent on the other side of the transaction) will go up because they'll think you might be trying to sneak something into the contract.

Listing agreements include a provision that the seller will cover any expenses incurred by the listing agent for photography, staging, advertising, and other expenses if the seller pulls out of the deal. I have rarely enforced that clause. Why? Because customers who want to break their agreement with us are unhappy customers for a reason. It means we didn't live up to their expectations. It happens—we aren't perfect and there have been times that we have gotten super busy or didn't have enough support staff to deliver the customer service we intended, we became overextended, and we let people down. This can happen when organizations, like mine, are slow to hire for the best long-term fit.

To me, it's all about doing the right thing and attempting to fix the customer service gap first, then being super transparent about whatever happened, taking ownership for any mistake we may have made, and ultimately, let the customer out of the contract if they still desire. Yes, I will lose money, but that's a business loss I'm willing to take. My reputation and relationship with the customer are more important to me than recouping a few thousand dollars in lost expenses and lost business revenue. Our company has the financial freedom to not be crippled by losing a couple of grand, and that's important because it gives you the ability to deliver your best customer service when you are financially stable and are able to keep those things from happening in the first place.

> ## Financial stability gives you freedom to make the right decisions.

Holding people to a contract only creates more animosity and tension during a transaction, no matter what kind of contract you're arguing about. I've had people come to me in the midst of a divorce, needing to refinance or sell their house as part of their divorce decree.

They argue over everything from who will stay in the home to the listing price. I remind them that the more they fight and the longer it takes to agree on all of the terms, the more money their attorneys make, meaning there's less money going into the divorcing spouses' pockets. It's even worse if they let a judge decide how things will be done because no one could agree. Nobody wants someone else to decide for them (in this case, a court) because there's a good chance they won't be happy with the decision, so make those choices yourself before someone else makes them for you.

LISTEN TO YOUR INNER VOICE

In some cases, you avoid the confrontation altogether by listening to your gut. If you have reservations going into any deal, you probably shouldn't do it at all. Ask yourself if you're being overly pessimistic or is your intuition telling you not to take that step?

If you still aren't sure, go to your mentors and advisors. From the outside looking in, other people can often see things you can't. That old saying about not being able to see the forest through the trees is true. Sometimes we are too close to a deal or too emotionally invested to see the wisest path. I remember going to the destination wedding of my closest friend. I could just see something wasn't quite right and there was a little hesitation, outside of the normal nervous "I'm getting married" jitters and told her that she didn't have to go through with the wedding. There was another couple there with us and I remember telling the bride-to-be that we could just turn this into a vacation instead and if she still wanted to get married later, we could come back and make it official next year. In the end, she walked down the aisle but the marriage ultimately ended up in a bitter divorce that cost her thousands of dollars. Talk about a nightmare, followed by multiple restraining orders.

Remember, insight is God's whisper of direction. If things are going south or you are unsure in *any* way, walk away before it gets worse.

> Don't be afraid to turn a potential disaster into a party and avoid costly legal battles.

When I first started *Tampa Home Talk*, I went to many of the businesses my company had supported over the years to ask about sponsorships because I was personally covering the airtime. Nowadays, radio costs are offset by sponsors. You start out covering all your own costs, then begin exchanging advertising and promotion for sponsorship.

I was surprised at how many businesses didn't want to write a check and give back in an effort for both of our businesses to grow but there was not a lot of selflessness coming from the other side. I started looking into the business we sent their way and calculated how much they were making in revenue based on our patronage. We pulled our business from some because we weren't interested in one-way relationships. There was a lot of give, give, give, but we were getting nothing in return. It's true that some of our relationships changed when they chose not to support us in return. The irony is that two of the people ended up closing up shop and working for the sponsors we decided to partner with for the show.

> That old adage is true: you can go fast alone but you can go farther and wider with others.

If your business does business with other companies, look at what percentage of your revenue is comes from that relationship. How does their company impact you and your growth? Are you returning that support in an equal way? Whether that is a financial exchange or simply by referring them with new prospective clients, or if are you just taking their support and not expressing gratitude—say *thank you* and do more to help them grow in return.

LEARN TO SAY THANK YOU

As I started examining my own business relationships, I realized how many people helped me grow by referring people to me all the time. I wanted to show them my appreciation by giving them what they needed, which could be anything from a referral to a great car dealer who will not take advantage of them or to an electrician that could help them with something at home so that they don't have to find people via some random Google search. This is also where my idea for Client Appreciation parties came from. We had bigger bashes for our clients and then smaller, more intimate gatherings for VIPs who deserved a little extra attention. I wanted them to know how grateful I was for their support by giving them one very precious commodity—my time.

As you grow older and wiser, time becomes a *really* precious resource. A busy business owner juggles many balls and has to be cognizant of how much time he or she gives to everyone, including family. Sometimes that means restructuring your priorities. Every year, during business planning, I've made a conscious choice to look at my numbers and see what percentage of business comes from where and then decide where I should focus my efforts, resources, and gratitude.

On the opposite side of the coin, we can't be afraid to follow-up and ask how a customer's overall experience was with us and how things are going, as well as see what they need now that they are settled into their home. We make it a point to talk to our clients three months after their closing. Because of this check-in, we found out that a home inspector we recommended had missed some major things he shouldn't have. Once can be a mistake, but two or three different big misses is a cause for us to seek a new home inspector relationship to whom we will refer our clients.

Some agents might prefer a home inspector who doesn't make waves and who helps purchases go smoothly by glossing over problems, but that's not how I allow myself or my business to operate. From the buyer's perspective, I would never want to be the buyer making the largest purchase of my life, only to later discover my agent allowed something like that to go on. This just isn't going to happen on my watch.

We have a ninety-day "Love Where You Live Guarantee" and we expect everyone who works for us and with us to deliver on that promise. We try to check in regularly with our customers. One of the downsides to all our growth is that I don't get to make as many of those post-purchase personal follow-up calls as I would like. I don't want a customer to think, even for a minute, that I don't care about them or that we don't have their best interests at heart, ALWAYS.

> We're not just in it for the money.
> If that were the case, I'd already be long gone.

HAVE A PLAN AND A COACH

I see it all the time—a business that's trying to grow but doesn't have a business plan or any kind of regular measuring analytics to track its progress and numbers on a consistent basis, as well as a year-end review. You need this information to be successful. If you don't have it, you can't prepare for the future, correct mistakes, redirect money to areas not producing a return on your investment, nor can you ensure you are maximizing profits. I know agents who sell more than I do and who are recognized on a national stage for their volume and growth—yet they aren't profitable.

Why would you put yourself through all that stress and extra headaches only to end up running in the red? That doesn't pay the bills, nor does it help you get to where you want to go. You need a plan to help you get from Point A to Point B and you need information to make informed decisions and allow for any detours you may need to take along the way. It's like getting in your car saying you want to go to Canada and just driving aimlessly!

You need at least a basic plan. You need to know the route you will take, have a back-up plan if roads are closed, how long it will take to get there, how often you will need to stop, and how much money you'll need for gas and food. A planner asks a lot of questions in advance to map out a great trip. Being strategic in your planning allows you to maximize your time, effort, resources, and money. In the end, a great plan will help you go further faster, while also learning what not to do if you make the trip again.

Professional athletes don't show up to a game without a strategic plan for winning and they don't play without a coach. Professional business people shouldn't either. Once you have had an amazing coach, you know the value they bring and I wouldn't dream of not having a coach. I've heard people say that coaching is an occupation for people who couldn't make it in the real world. To that, I say *you're interviewing the wrong people.*

Over the years, I have had many coaches and I can tell you that they are not all the same. I have a couple of coaches in my space who have significant accomplishments in their past. They have been successful and have earned the ability and right to coach me because they have already been where I want to go.

You should make them interview for the job of being your coach. Some of the questions you may want to consider asking a coach before you hire them are:

1. What is your background? What was your career path? What kind of success have you had in and outside of my industry that qualifies you as a coach? Tell me about your success.

2. How have you helped other people/teams grow? To what extent? Let's talk numbers and make sure you have worked with other people who have achieved the success I want for myself and my business.

3. How transparent are you? Are you going to ask me the hard questions about things we need to discuss? A great coach will tell you the truth, even when you don't want to hear it.

4. Will you give me deadlines and have certain expectation for me and hold me accountable for each goal?

5. How do you plan to hold me accountable? What happens if I let you down? What if you let me down?

6. Are there other people you have coached who had goals similar to my own? Can I can call him/her/them for a reference?

7. Why are you a coach? What are some of your big life goals?

8. My coach will make sure I'm focused and can see when I'm missing something. Ashley has a way of ripping off the band-aid and diving in. It's perfect for someone like me.

KEYS TO SUCCESS

It pays to be prepared for any eventuality. Staying ahead of disaster is as simple as:

- Saving money
- Always have reserves
- Always look for new opportunities
- Assess all risks before jumping into anything

If there is discomfort in any of these conversations, GOOD! That means you are both going in the right direction together.

My coach's job is to poke holes in things I'm doing and help me discover what isn't working. They will tell you the truth, as well as challenge you and your thinking. A coach encourages you when you are down or have a rough week and is there to challenge you to look at everything from your expenses, both cash in hand and in resources used, to hires, and also to know your big vision.

I'm also a firm believer in mastermind groups. There's a saying that the five people you hang around with the most are the ones who influence you the most. You can easily tell someone's net worth, thought process, and more because it will be the average of their closest circle. I chose to surround myself with successful, positive people because I grew up with a lot of negativity and none of the "privilege" one might *think* I had growing up, from the outside looking in anyway. I chose healthy relationships in my spouse, friendships, and in business because I knew that was how I would grow.

I am a part of several different mastermind groups, where we connect on different subjects at different times, whether it's building wealth or strategizing promotions. We share information because we all have the same goal—to help each other grow and expand. A good mastermind group is that rising tide floating all the boats, not just one or two.

My mastermind group has been a great brainstorming resource when I've needed creative solutions to problems. One time, I had a customer who wanted to buy a piece of land but knew it would be extremely difficult to get a mortgage from a traditional bank for undeveloped land. The seller already had a note on the land and wasn't in a position to hold a note for the new buyer. My mastermind group collaborated on assessing the risk of lending money to the buyer myself. I had the cash available and knew I would make a healthy return on my investment—better than traditional bank interest, which in today's age, is almost zero. Everyone won in that situation. The seller was able to get out from the burden of the payments, the private investor holding the current mortgage got the payoff he needed, and the buyer got the property they wanted and the money they needed via a private loan. By funding it, I was able to take advantage of a new type of opportunity, as well as earn interest on the mortgage.

> Be ready to shift gears and embrace new opportunities whenever they arise. Don't forget that you always need to be on the lookout for great opportunities.

CHAPTER TEN

HAPPILY EVER AFTER

This chapter is where things get exciting. Once you've done all the work of finding, building, and sealing the perfect relationships with your customers, you're undoubtedly going to want everything to last. In marriages, that happy- ever-after ending takes a lot of work, communication, and compromise. It's no different in business.

ESTABLISH THE FOUNDATION

Stability is the base of any long-term happy ending. For many people, that stability comes from owning a house. According to a Federal Reserve study done in 2016, the median net worth of a homeowner increased from about $200,000 to $231,400 while the median net worth of a renter decreased by 5% to $5,200. In our country, we have endless mortgage programs and home loan options for homebuyers with as low as a zero-down payment.

Unlike some countries that require people to put 50% (or more) down or pay cash for the full amount of their home (which can take decades to save), there are many great programs here in the United States. In many cases, other countries have multi-generational housing, where kids, parents, and grandparents all live together and the home passes down from one generation to the next because people often can't afford to get a home of their own due to the lack of affordable mortgage options, and even affordable housing prices.

Once you own a home, you are on track to begin building generational wealth. Your home is not just a place to live—it's a way to give you options for investments and growth. When I look back at my very first home mortgage payment in 1996, I paid $82,000 for the home and had a $658 a month payment on a fifteen-year mortgage. If I bought that same home today, even with lower interest rates, it would cost at least double what it did twenty years ago. The home price would be in the mid to low $200,000s for that same home. I paid $82,000 for it;, imagine what that will be worth in another twenty years?

You don't want to be house poor. You simply want to secure and control your housing costs by buying, because once you get your house payment settled it's not going to change very much. For instance, my mother's first house payment, was only $316 a month, and she paid $35,000 for it in 1988. We sold this home in 2016 for $110,000 to an all-cash buyer but only for the value of the land because they were tearing the house down and building a new home in its place. When you do the math on the payments she made and the time value of money, she couldn't even rent a bedroom in someone's house for that price a month. Her housing costs were always predictable and affordable because she had a mortgage. Homeownership is the only way you can secure your housing costs.

With most of us, even if we have a thirty-year mortgage, your home could be paid off, assuming you didn't refinance or use the house as an ATM machine by constantly refinancing or leveraging your equity. Once the mortgage is paid off, all you are left with are taxes and the insurance on a free and clear home that you can now rent out for passive income per month.

You don't need to buy bigger and better every time you move. You want to weigh all the factors—time, value, and money— when you make a housing purchase. A great rule of thumb is to keep your housing payment at 25% of your income. So, if you made $100,000 per year, you would keep your housing payment around $2,100. If you make $50,000 keep your payment around $1,100 per month—and so on and so forth. You want to allow yourself some grace to be able to build some savings and have an ample emergency fund should you lose your job or something unexpected happens.

I also try to pay my mortgage ahead by at least one or two months and then continue making every monthly payment. This takes a lot of pressure off should you lose your job, have a sudden loss of income, or a big expense. By making extra payments, you are accelerating the payment on the mortgage principal. Even paying one extra payment per year or compounding interest on a bi-weekly payment plan, your thirty-year mortgage becomes a twenty-three-year mortgage without having to pay an extra dime for the house. If you are young and you are reading this, I promise those years will go by faster than you think—just ask your parents!

> If you want true generational wealth, start with that foundation of a home and use it to build your bank account. If you are a parent reading this, tell your kids!

If I had to do it all over again, I would have bought a multifamily home—a duplex, triplex, or quadruplex (four-unit home). I would have lived in one of those units and rented out the others. That way, the tenants' rent pays your mortgage, enough to have the house completely paid off in less than ten years. Now you have a totally debt-free asset that is *making* you money. Concentrate on paying down the mortgage as fast as possible. If you were paying $1100.00 in rent, keep that same payment and your tenants' money going into the "home account". Use this "home account" only for mortgage payments for that property and your tenants' rent. That's the very definition of cash flow. Even if you account for repairs, as long as you aren't spending the rental income elsewhere, you will come out ahead.

The challenge I see with young people today is that they want what their parents have and they want it right now.

They want the big, nice house with the pool and fenced yard, but they forget it took their parents twenty to thirty years to buy that kind of house, maybe even after trading up several times. Young adults should take a step back and be more conservative in their approach to home ownership so that they can be millionaires sooner down the road, than later. After all, money gives you options, and *lots* of them!

THE TWO-YEAR MILLIONAIRE PLAN

You want to become a millionaire? Don't you? Who wouldn't, right? It's absolutely possible, regardless of your upbringing or even your current socioeconomic status. You just have to be smart with your money and investments, and have a plan, and review that plan regularly. Here are some tips that can help you if you are planning to buy your first home or even if you already own a home.

- Save 15% of your income and don't spend it unless it's on something that **makes you money**. Don't buy a car or a boat or anything with an engine or wheels—only use that 15% savings for wealth building (something that will return your money)

- Buy a smaller starter home or a multi-family home. After two years, rent it and buy the next house, pulling the down payment from that 15% you have been saving. Two years later, rent the second one and buy a third, and so on and so forth. Conservatively, in less than ten years you will have net worth of more than a million dollars.

- Don't wait for the market to fall. The reality is housing prices are going up and they're going to *keep* going up long term. There was a brief moment in 2010 when prices dipped enough that you could buy a house for the same price someone might have paid a decade earlier, but then REIT (Real Estate Investment Trust) money flooded the market and snatched up those properties. That window won't open again. Any other drops you see in prices will be normal cyclical real estate dips. Look at many opportunities before you jump to ensure you are getting the best deal using comparable home sales and factoring in costs for any repairs or updates.

- When you have a lot of properties, hire a property manager to take care of them so you don't have the day-to-day headaches of tenants calling to fix things, renew leases, and the many other calls that landlords will get who have more than a few rental properties. You may go crazy fielding all of these calls while also trying to do your primary day job.

- Consider doing a 1031 exchange, which is a tax-free way to sell those properties and invest them in another. This property exchange allows you to sell your property and buy something similar, like an apartment building, in an area that will soon be booming. Then you can keep on making money and pass that on to your kids—all tax-free. Of course, I can't give you legal or tax advice in this book, so make sure you arm yourself with a great team!

- Hire a super savvy CPA, financial advisor, real estate agent, and top-notch attorneys that are well versed in asset protection as well as real estate and landlord/tenant laws. Don't get so busy that you forget to review things with them regularly as laws, finances, and situations change. This helps make sure you are protected.

Some of the wealthiest people in the world make their money through real estate. It's not the only way but it's the best way, in my opinion. There's not as much risk in real estate as there is in something like the stock market. With real estate, you always have something tangible you can sell if you need to. It's not a liquid asset, but it's an appreciating asset, and it can be sold.

SURROUND YOURSELF WITH AMAZING PEOPLE

It's no fun to accumulate wealth and be alone the rest of your life. You won't grow or change unless you surround yourself with people who are smarter than you. Talent is surrounded by people who want to learn, grow, and maybe even want to groom someone to take over their job. To me, that's a compliment and a legacy. I want to encourage and inspire others to follow in my footsteps and make sure my business becomes a legacy that doesn't die when I do.

One of my coaches, Ashley, was an amazing Realtor® who stopped producing real estate to help others. To become the best you can be, read incessantly. Be a lifelong learner. Focus on the greater good you can do for the world and not just yourself. Give back as much as has been given to you. Gary Keller says, "People have lived before you, learn from them, stand on the shoulders of giants." Learn from others who know more than you do about something and give back to others with the expert knowledge you have to offer.

When I give people advice, it's not from a place of meeting *my* needs—it's about meeting *their needs*. I have an abundance mentality, so I'm not counting every penny in every interaction. When you operate from a place like that, it doesn't get in the way of the advice you give someone else.

KNOW WHEN TO LET GO

I'm still very much involved in my business, but I know that, one day, I will have to let go and hand the reins to someone else. So many business owners struggle with letting go. They resist growing toward moving on and stepping aside, or even taking on a different role, like CEO.

> Hire the right people now so you can step away later.

It's important to hire the people who can continue your legacy and know your vision. If you don't, what happens if something happens to you? Is all the good that you did and everything you believe in going to end up flushed down the toilet because there's no one left to run it? You have to put the right people in place if you want your legacy to continue. The bottom line is anything can happen to anyone at any time. Operating agreements are crucial, so have one.

My friend's father was an eye doctor who had to leave his practice after he got ill. We talked about how so many great professionals like her dad gave their lives to serve their clients and do it at a high level. However, once he left the business, it was done. Had he been continuously searching for talent, he could not only have grown his practice and mentored a new young doctor, but the right person could also have purchased his practice and continued to serve his patients. Now there is no real legacy of this thirty-year practice and all of his patients had to find a new doctor.

In real estate, we call that group of people who are learning and building the business behind you a Seventh Level Team. With this model, the business can run without you involved in everything because you are leaving it in the hands of smart people you can trust. That exit strategy is a proven model that works—and it makes sense to follow something that has a strong success rate.

If you hire the right people, the bigger you grow, and the better the talent that you attract, which ultimately makes the entire company stronger. A lot of business owners, myself included, have trouble taking that step back and letting the talent take the lead. At a certain point, you can't have everyone reporting to you because you can't do and be everywhere all the time. I had to learn this one the hard way! Trust the people you have put in place and believe they are going to do a great job.

Expect them to succeed—train them up in a strong culture and watch them grow.

If you are a solopreneur, then make a list of all those tasks you don't like to do (but have to) and all the things you love to do. Then find someone who loves to do the tasks you avoid. I don't like handling the accounting in my business, although I know how to do it. It's smarter for me to find someone who will do it efficiently and faster and do a better job than I ever will, so I look for that talent and, in the end, both parties come out of the relationship stronger.

REMEMBER ONE THING

I'm going to hammer this point because if you don't remember anything in this book about building relationships, I want you to at least remember this. I truly believe the fastest way to build wealth and succeed personally and professionally is this:

> No matter whether you are a mailman or the CEO of a Fortune 500 company, save 15% of your income for wealth building.

When people start doing this and see how much that account starts growing, it's really tempting to go buy a new boat or car. However, people with a high net worth think differently about money. They see it as a means to opportunities, not consumption.

For instance, when I give my kids money for chores, I talk to them about what to do with the money. *You can take this five dollar bill and spend it or you can take two dollars of the five and figure out how to make that two dollars turn into five dollars.* Teaching them early to save and look for opportunities to make money will give them the financial freedom later in life that most adults in this country need desperately right now. Too often, people today get hung up in the rat race and end up too tired at the end of a long day to even "think" about new opportunities.

I had a client who was a UPS driver. He owned fifteen different properties. He was a simple guy who bought one property, then another, in the way I shared above, and through that, he became successful. He saved for retirement and had a pension with UPS but he also saved 15-20% of his income and was able to buy his next rental property every two years. He kept an eye out and when the right opportunity came up, he would buy it. Now he makes enough in passive income that he won't see a dip in income when he is ready to retire.

One of the things Dave Ramsey says is: *Broke people ask how much this will cost per month and rich people ask* **how much it will cost**. There is a mindset shift there that, quite frankly, most Americans still have not figured out. For instance, look at a classic millionaire—they understand how numbers work and know that for every dollar they don't pay in interest frees that money to be invested elsewhere. Think about that! Look at your last mortgage statement and go to the line that says "interest". Go on, do it... I'll wait... Now how much is that?

Shocked? What could you buy with that amount of money if you saved that amount for a year? Five years?

When you start thinking differently about money, you make different choices. You begin to realize that you could pay $400 a month for a car payment, with a good chunk of that going toward interest, or save that $400 every month and use the almost $5,000 you amass at the end of the year to buy a car for cash. You have no debt and you can trade up every year or so until you have the car you want if you keep saving—without needing a loan or paying interest.

Earlier in this book, I shared about how I got bad accounting advice when I first started my business and wound up, at twenty-five years old, owing over $25,000 in payroll taxes. An IRS agent came knocking on my door. I was pregnant with my first child and scared out of my mind! Interest rates had started to creep up to over 8% and to say we were living paycheck to paycheck with tens of thousands in credit card debt would be an understatement. Thank God the IRS lady took pity on me and helped me get on a repayment plan and abated some of the penalties. I don't think most people would be so lucky. This experience, one of the worst, was also one of the best life lessons ever. I just had to be willing to look for the lesson and make changes.

KEYS TO SUCCESS

BASIC KEYS TO A GREAT RELATIONSHIP WITH ANYONE

- Get to know that person on a deep level; why are they here? What do they need and want at a deep level?
- Use that clarity to make all the decisions and choices easier.
- Care deeply about the other person, and what they need and want.
- Be selfless and give more than you take.
- ABC: **A**lways **B**e **C**ommunicating. People love communication.
- Have transparency and admit when you are wrong.
- Never operate from a place of need or ulterior motives.

Even now, I can remember not being able to sleep at night because of the surmounting debt that was a never-ending cycle. When that happened, I started reading everything I could about money and I decided, right then and there, that I was never going to live like that EVER AGAIN. If I wanted to end up in a different place financially, I couldn't do what everyone else was doing and have what everyone else "appeared" to have. I had to worry about me and my house.

Put that 15% into the bank and forget about it. Make savings a little competition with yourself, if that helps motivate you. Start seeking investment opportunities. Never buy anything that goes down in value—instead look for things that legitimately make money like properties. Above all, do your research before investing any of your hard-earned money.

> When you change your relationship with money, you change your other relationships too.

If my business has a bad month, I will be the last person to get paid. I'm more concerned with keeping my talented people than getting a paycheck that month. None of the advice I have given in this book or to anyone I mentor comes from a place of need. I don't have to worry about money because I have worked very hard to remain financially stable and debt free. I call this place contentment.

That's the true key to happy relationships in all parts of your life—financial security. You don't end up friends with, married to, or in business with anyone because you are broke. If you are standing on stable financial ground, your stress is lower, your decision-making is less panicked, and you can take the time to invest in your business, yourself, and the people around you.

Start today by investing in yourself, by reading books and learning. Then invest in your business by working on it—not just in it—and invest in the relationships you have with your customers, vendors, partners, sphere of influence. Work from a mentality of abundance and gratitude and you will find that those relationships blossom naturally and build upon one another. You will never have to pick up the phone and make another cold call—because you'll be surrounded by customers and people who love to work with you!

Not to mention I am sure you will love them too.

> All relationships in life are better and flow naturally if you can focus on your people and their needs and not the money.

So why did I write this whole book about relationships and selling? Because all of these pieces and stories are what got me where I am today. These life-learning lessons have helped me build wealth and sell thousands of homes to customers who love and trust me. My team and I don't take this lightly. It all started with being more interested in their needs and having a genuine heart of a teacher to then understand their perspective and lead them where they want to go.

Love your people. Let them know how much you care and the results will follow

> And always, love where you live! 🖤

Jeremy Farner's house, one of my early mortgage and real estate clients.

I was featured in *Real Producers Magazine* in front of a client's home that we sold. We met that client because they were a listener of *Tampa Home Talk*, my weekly radio show.

Jeremy J. Farner

January 18, 2006

Ms. Katrina Madewell
KMI Mortgage
3111 W MLK Jr Blvd
Suite 100
Tampa, FL 33607

Ms. Madewell,

First, thank you for your efforts and thank your staff for theirs in this endeavor, my first home purchase. From the beginning you have set a bar FAR above what I expected and have truly earned my referral and accolades to anyone who is in the market for a home/mortgage. Chrissy (sorry if I spelled in wrong) and the rest of your staff are direct representatives of your dedication and effort. They are to be commended for their tireless and I am sure unsung work. THANK YOU ALL!

On a personal note, I wanted to let you know that I have set up my mortgage payments through my bank to be made every 4 weeks. I would appreciate your comments as I have attached a list of when the payments will be made. I also look forward to rolling the second mortgage into a home equity line after six months. I am sure that that will be a MUCH easier task.

Finally, you are welcome in my home anytime, just call first! I thought you would like to know that you are the first to receive a letter with my NEW address and phone number on it. I felt that it is an honor that you have earned and deserve. Again, thank you and your staff for all of your efforts...and I look forward to working with you in the future...

Personal "thank you"
note from Jeremy Farner.

Hosting *Tampa Home Talk.*

135

My mother's first house.

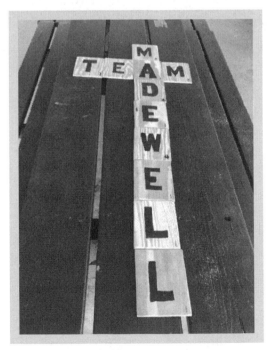

Our outdoor, oversized Scrabble game.
Our team put this together after one of our client parties.

Amy George, my producer Pat's wife,
hanging with one of the kids at our annual picnic in the park.

Jenny and Melvin, my dear clients who had the courage to tell me about a bad hire.

Since I don't process loans anymore,
Sarah Crickey has been my lender and is now one of my best friends.

Pat George my producer
MCing our picnic in the park.

Carl and Margie, parents of
my longtime friend (and like
my own). They owned their
house for 38 years and I had
the honor of selling it.

Our very own Christmas Cheer Squad!

My husband Chris who gives me so much so thatI can succeed, I love you.

TampaHomeTalk.com

Our mission for *Tampa Home Talk* is to help people keep and maintain great credit, live within their means, and build wealth.

- Connect with us on Facebook for the weekly livestream of *Tampa Home Talk* on Fridays, from 8am-10 am EST
- Subscribe to the podcast of our past shows: TampaHomeTalk.com/radio
- Subscribe to our YouTube channel at: YouTube.com/KMadewel
- Follow us on Twitter, LinkedIn, and Facebook: @TampaHomeTalk

If you are or have the perfect guest for the show, email us at: radio@tampahometalk.com

KATRINA MADEWELL KELLER WILLIAMS REALTY
5020 W. Linebaugh Ave, Suite 100 Tampa, FL 33624

With every transaction, we deliver on our **Love Where You Live 90-Day Guarantee**. Work with us and see what a difference experience makes.

Because your home is your biggest asset, liability, and monthly payment, you can count on our team to deliver the best advice and treat your money like it's our own! Your success is our success.

If you have ever considered a career in real estate and love the concept of selling through relationships, reach out to us at:

RealEstateCareersTampa.com/join-our-team

CONTACT KATRINA FOR SOME GREAT FREE RESOURCES, INCLUDING:

- *The Room by Room Tips for Getting Top Dollar When You Sell Your Home*

- *How to Get More than the Asking Price Every Time*

Facebook: @YourTampaRealtor

LinkedIn: @TampaHomesKatrina

Twitter: @TampaHomes

Instagram: @TampaHomes

Pinterest: @TampaHomes

ABOUT THE AUTHOR

Katrina Madewell, radio show host of *Tampa Home Talk*, has been in the real estate industry for nearly three decades. She is consistently ranked in the top 5% of Realtors in Tampa Bay for sales and has a 90% repeat and referral rate with her clients. She is committed to helping people love where they live while also teaching others how to build wealth through real estate. A native Tampa resident, Katrina has been married for more than two decades and is a mom of four uniquely amazing kids.

Made in the USA
Columbia, SC
23 January 2021